1-95
17.00
B&T
VER

W9-BKX-009

HM
1E1
.184 7 Cultu Whitehead, Fred   28501
.A1   Culture wars
C87
1994

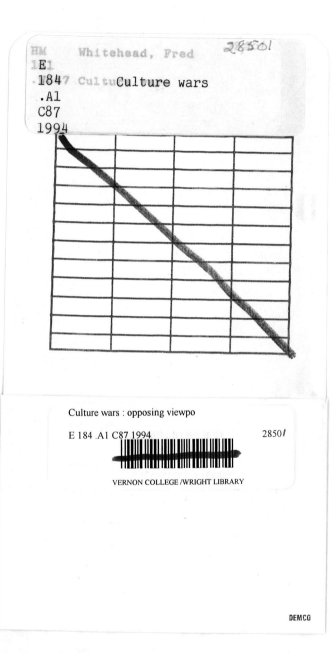

Culture wars : opposing viewpo

E 184 .A1 C87 1994   28501

VERNON COLLEGE /WRIGHT LIBRARY

DEMCO

CULTURE WARS

WARS

OPPOSING VIEWPOINTS®

Other Books of Related Interest in the Opposing Viewpoints Series:

American Values
American Government
America's Future
Censorship
Christopher Columbus and His Legacy
Constructing a Life Philosophy
Education in America
The Family in America
Homosexuality
Immigration
The Mass Media
Racism in America
Religion in America
Science & Religion
Sexual Values
Social Justice
Teenage Sexuality

CULTURE WARS

WARS

OPPOSING VIEWPOINTS

David Bender & Bruno Leone, *Series Editors*

Fred Whitehead, University of Kansas, *Book Editor*

OPPOSING
VIEWPOINTS
SERIES®

Greenhaven Press, Inc.   PO Box 289009   San Diego, CA 92198-9009

VERNON REGIONAL
JUNIOR COLLEGE LIBRARY

No part of this book may be reproduced or used in any form or by any means, electrical, mechanical, or otherwise, including, but not limited to, photocopy, recording, or any information storage and retrieval system, without prior written permission from the publisher.

Library of Congress Cataloging-in-Publication Data

Culture wars : opposing viewpoints / Fred Whitehead, book editor.
    p.   cm. — (Opposing viewpoints series)
  Includes bibliographical references and index.
  Summary: Presents opposing viewpoints on issues related to cultural diversity, American education, cultural values, and the decay of American culture.
  ISBN 1-56510-101-4 (lib. bdg. : alk. paper) — ISBN 1-56510-100-6 (pbk. : alk. paper)
  1. Pluralism (Social sciences) — United States. 2. Multiculturalism — United States. 3. United States — Civilization. [1. Multiculturalism.] I. Whitehead, Fred. II. Series: Opposing viewpoints series (Unnumbered)
E184.A1C87   1994
306'.0973—dc20   93-8512
                                        CIP
                                        AC

Copyright © 1994 by Greenhaven Press, Inc.
Printed in the U.S.A.

"Congress shall make no law . . .
abridging the freedom of speech,
or of the press."

First Amendment to the U.S. Constitution

The basic foundation of our democracy is the first amendment
guarantee of freedom of expression. The Opposing Viewpoints
Series is dedicated to the concept of this basic freedom and the
idea that it is more important to practice it than to enshrine it.

Contents

Why Consider Opposing Viewpoints?

"The only way in which a human being can make some approach to knowing the whole of a subject is by hearing what can be said about it by persons of every variety of opinion and studying all modes in which it can be looked at by every character of mind. No wise man ever acquired his wisdom in any mode but this."

John Stuart Mill

In our media-intensive culture it is not difficult to find differing opinions. Thousands of newspapers and magazines and dozens of radio and television talk shows resound with differing points of view. The difficulty lies in deciding which opinion to agree with and which "experts" seem the most credible. The more inundated we become with differing opinions and claims, the more essential it is to hone critical reading and thinking skills to evaluate these ideas. Opposing Viewpoints books address this problem directly by presenting stimulating debates that can be used to enhance and teach these skills. The varied opinions contained in each book examine many different aspects of a single issue. While examining these conveniently edited opposing views, readers can develop critical thinking skills such as the ability to compare and contrast authors' credibility, facts, argumentation styles, use of persuasive techniques, and other stylistic tools. In short, the Opposing Viewpoints Series is an ideal way to attain the higher-level thinking and reading skills so essential in a culture of diverse and contradictory opinions.

In addition to providing a tool for critical thinking, Opposing Viewpoints books challenge readers to question their own strongly held opinions and assumptions. Most people form their opinions on the basis of upbringing, peer pressure, and personal, cultural, or professional bias. By reading carefully balanced opposing views, readers must directly confront new ideas as well as the opinions of those with whom they disagree. This is not to simplistically argue that everyone who reads opposing views will—or should—change his or her opinion. Instead, the series enhances readers' depth of understanding of their own views by encouraging confrontation with opposing ideas. Careful examination of others' views can lead to the readers' understanding of the logical inconsistencies in their own opinions, perspective on why they hold an opinion, and the consideration of the possibility that their opinion requires further evaluation.

Evaluating Other Opinions

To ensure that this type of examination occurs, Opposing Viewpoints books present all types of opinions. Prominent spokespeople on different sides of each issue as well as well-known professionals from many disciplines challenge the reader. An additional goal of the series is to provide a forum for other, less known, or even unpopular viewpoints. The opinion of an ordinary person who has had to make the decision to cut off life support from a terminally ill relative, for example, may be just as valuable and provide just as much insight as a medical ethicist's professional opinion. The editors have two additional purposes in including these less known views. One, the editors encourage readers to respect others' opinions—even when not enhanced by professional credibility. It is only by reading or listening to and objectively evaluating others' ideas that one can determine whether they are worthy of consideration. Two, the inclusion of such viewpoints encourages the important critical thinking skill of objectively evaluating an author's credentials and bias. This evaluation will illuminate an author's reasons for taking a particular stance on an issue and will aid in readers' evaluation of the author's ideas.

As series editors of the Opposing Viewpoints Series, it is our hope that these books will give readers a deeper understanding of the issues debated and an appreciation of the complexity of even seemingly simple issues when good and honest people disagree. This awareness is particularly important in a democratic society such as ours in which people enter into public debate to determine the common good. Those with whom one disagrees should not be regarded as enemies but rather as people whose views deserve careful examination and may shed light on one's own.

Thomas Jefferson once said that "difference of opinion leads to inquiry, and inquiry to truth." Jefferson, a broadly educated man, argued that "if a nation expects to be ignorant and free . . . it expects what never was and never will be." As individuals and as a nation, it is imperative that we consider the opinions of others and examine them with skill and discernment. The Opposing Viewpoints Series is intended to help readers achieve this goal.

David L. Bender & Bruno Leone,
Series Editors

Introduction

> *"The culture wars have provided us with a unique opportunity to re-examine the ideals of colleges and universities, and to answer the questions of what should be taught and how we ought to teach."*
>
> John K. Wilson, *Democratic Culture*, Spring 1993.

Every society has a culture—art in the broadest sense, including music, sculpture, literature, the cinema, and crafts such as textiles. Concepts of ethics, philosophy, and anthropology deal with systems of thought and beliefs, and also contribute to local, national, or continental definitions of culture. A culture's art and beliefs can be an enormously stabilizing force, providing continuity and a reassuring system to those who live in a particular society. Some societies, such as those of ancient India, China, and Egypt, are notable for long periods of dynastic order that provided unity. But in the modern world, a combination of factors has led to tension and conflict inside cultures, and with other competing cultures. In advanced industrialized countries, long accepted religious and cultural beliefs have clashed with a concentration on "the things of this world"—the benefits of a secular, materialist society.

There have been many cultural conflicts in history, but the modern use of the term "culture war" originates in late nineteenth-century Germany, where the statesman Otto von Bismarck engaged in a *kultur-krieg*—a bitter struggle to restrict the authority and political power of the Catholic church. In twentieth-century America, culture wars have sometimes occurred around religious issues, such as the famous Scopes trial of 1925, where a young science teacher in Tennessee was convicted for the crime of advocating the theory of evolution in his classes. The Scopes trial was widely viewed as a watershed, for even though Scopes was convicted, his fine was small, and the pro-science forces claimed a moral victory. In the trial, literal interpretations of the Bible were revealed as fallacious on the witness stand. Subsequently, Fundamentalist Christianity passed through decades of near-withdrawal from public life. During the

1960s and 1970s, religion as a cultural influence appeared to decline, and other events led to radical changes in how Americans perceived themselves and their culture. The fight for civil rights among American blacks challenged the way many whites viewed minorities. During the Vietnam War, Americans questioned their government's policies and morality. And, finally, the Watergate affair seemed to destroy faith in presidential authority and power.

In the 1980s, however, a resurgence of conservatism, the weakness of liberal policies, and economic troubles including a high deficit culminated in the election of Ronald Reagan. Reagan openly advocated a more conservative approach to culture, and as a broad majority of voters elected him, Reagan touched a sympathetic nerve in the nation. Reagan appointees were unabashedly conservative in their views, and Reagan's stance against abortion and his willingness to bring other moral issues into the political arena changed the tenor of debate across the country.

In the late eighties, controversies over censorship, obscenity, pornography, and the definition of acceptable cultural standards dominated headlines, the courts, and college campuses. Among the debates that marked the rise of what has now come to be known as the "culture wars" was whether the federal government, through the National Endowment for the Arts, should have supported an exhibition of the work of Robert Mapplethorpe, whose photographs depicted explicit homosexual acts. Another controversy emerged over explicit rock lyrics dealing with sex, violence, and degradation of women, and whether such albums should contain a label warning parents of the music's explicit content. Across college campuses, disputes arose concerning the inclusion of more non-Western literature and teachings in the curriculum, to offset a perceived reliance on Western culture.

Because the government at all levels has been involved in these disputes, the culture wars have become intensely politicized. *Culture Wars: Opposing Viewpoints* examines present-day controversies in art and education in the following chapters: What Cultural Influences Should the United States Perpetuate? Are Diverse Traditions Fairly Represented in American Education? Is American Culture Decadent? and Should Government Enforce Cultural Values? Every issue covered in this book is intricately tied to Americans' sense of national identity, and to the various traditions that have contributed to that identity.

What Cultural Influences Should the United States Perpetuate?

Chapter Preface

One of the major controversial issues in the war over culture is whether America has an identifiable heritage that should influence current values and beliefs. Many people, such as educator Allan Bloom, believe that America's culture harkens from Western white European civilization, and that we are in danger of losing this tradition. These people see America's current path as one of loss of character and culture that can only be prevented by a return to the values of classical civilization. The great German poet Goethe once stated that there is no more horrible sight than ignorance in action, and this prospect, they believe, is now at hand in America.

Others, however, vehemently disagree with this picture of America as having a single, identifiable cultural definition to which it can return. They especially take issue with the idea that America's tradition should be identified as white, European, and Christian. They point out that the beliefs and values of early European colonists were quickly challenged by a myriad of different traditions. Native Americans, for example, had very different religions and cultures, as well as very different ideas of how to use the land. Later, other religious groups such as Quakers and Baptists sharply differed with the Puritans, and faced severe legal repression such as whipping, banishment, or even death. Before the Civil War, black slaves, although obviously oppressed, made important contributions to American culture in agriculture, music, food, and religion. During the years of western expansion, Hispanics also added to the cultural mix. And millions of immigrants have continued to change and alter America's culture. Many people argue that it is in this heritage of diverse religions and cultures that America should find its roots.

The authors in this chapter debate which cultural traditions have contributed most to the making of American culture, and which should serve as a guide to the nation's future.

VIEWPOINT

1

"Tradition . . . is lost when the voice of civilization elaborated over millennia has been stilled."

The Influence of Western Civilization Must Predominate

Allan Bloom

Contemporary American college and university students are, according to Allan Bloom, ignorant of and indifferent to the major intellectual and literary traditions of Western civilization. Without a deep knowledge of those traditions, he argues, young people in this country are doomed to a form of shallow driftlessness and moral instability. His book *The Closing of the American Mind* became a bestseller after its publication in 1987, and prompted a number of both supportive and critical responses in journals of literature and public opinion. At his death in 1992, Bloom was a professor of philosophy at the University of Chicago.

As you read, consider the following questions:

1. What does the author say is the typical student's attitude toward books? What kinds of books does he favor?
2. What, in Bloom's view, is "our most fatal tendency"?
3. What is Bloom's view of feminism and relativism? Why does he believe that they are responsible for a low state of culture?

From *The Closing of the American Mind* by Allan Bloom. Copyright © 1987 by Allan Bloom. Reprinted by permission of Simon & Schuster.

I have begun to wonder whether the experience of the greatest texts from early childhood is not a prerequisite for a concern throughout life for them and for lesser but important literature. The soul's longing, its intolerable irritation under the constraints of the conditional and limited, may very well require encouragement at the outset. At all events, whatever the cause, our students have lost the practice of and the taste for reading. They have not learned how to read, nor do they have the expectation of delight or improvement from reading. They are "authentic," as against the immediately preceding university generations, in having few cultural pretensions and in refusing hypocritical ritual bows to high culture.

When I first noticed the decline in reading during the late sixties, I began asking my large introductory classes, and any other group of younger students to which I spoke, what books really count for them. Most are silent, puzzled by the question. The notion of books as companions is foreign to them. Justice Hugo Black with his tattered copy of the Constitution in his pocket at all times is not an example that would mean much to them. There is no printed word to which they look for counsel, inspiration or joy. Sometimes one student will say "the Bible." (He learned it at home, and his Biblical studies are not usually continued at the university.) There is always a girl who mentions Ayn Rand's *The Fountainhead*, a book, although hardly literature, which, with its sub-Nietzschean assertiveness, excites somewhat eccentric youngsters to a new way of life. A few students mention recent books that struck them and supported their own self-interpretation, like *The Catcher in the Rye*. (Theirs is usually the most genuine response and also shows a felt need for help in self-interpretation. But it is an uneducated response. Teachers should take advantage of the need expressed in it to show such students that better writers can help them more.) After such sessions I am pursued by a student or two who wants to make it clear that he or she is really influenced by books, not just by one or two but by many. Then he recites a list of classics he may have grazed in high school.

A Lack of Understanding

Imagine such a young person walking through the Louvre or the Uffizi, and you can immediately grasp the condition of his soul. In his innocence of the stories of Biblical and Greek or Roman antiquity, Raphael, Leonardo, Michelangelo, Rembrandt and all the others can say nothing to him. All he sees are colors and forms—modern art. In short, like almost everything else in his spiritual life, the paintings and statues are abstract. No matter what much of modern wisdom asserts, these artists counted on immediate recognition of their subjects and, what is more, on their having a powerful meaning for their viewers. The works were the fulfillment of those meanings, giving them a sensuous reality and hence completing them. Without those meanings, and without their being something essential to the viewer as a moral, political and religious being, the works lose their essence. It is not merely the tradition that is lost when the voice of civilization elaborated over millennia has been stilled in this way. It is being itself that vanishes beyond the dissolving horizon. One of the most flattering things that ever happened to me as a teacher occurred when I received a postcard from a very good student on his first visit to Italy, who wrote, "You are not a professor of political philosophy but a travel agent." Nothing could have better expressed my intention as an educator. He thought I had prepared him to see. Then he could begin thinking for himself with something to think about. The real sensation of the Florence in which Machiavelli is believable is worth all the formulas of metaphysics ten times over. Education in our times must try to find whatever there is in students that might yearn for completion, and to reconstruct the learning that would enable them autonomously to seek that completion.

In a less grandiose vein, students today have nothing like the Dickens who gave so many of us the unforgettable Pecksniffs, Micawbers, Pips, with which we sharpened our vision, allowing us some subtlety in our distinction of human types. It is a complex set of experiences that enables one to say so simply, "He is a Scrooge." Without literature, no such observations are possible and the fine art of comparison is lost. The psychological obtuseness of our students is appalling, because they have only pop psychology to tell them what people are like, and the range of their motives. As the awareness that we owed almost exclusively to literary genius falters, people become more alike, for want of knowing they can be otherwise. What poor substitutes for real diversity are the wild rainbows of dyed hair and other external differences that tell the observer nothing about what is inside.

Lack of education simply results in students' seeking for enlightenment wherever it is readily available, without being able to distinguish between the sublime and trash, insight and propaganda. . . .

The Myth of the Here and Now

The failure to read good books both enfeebles the vision and strengthens our most fatal tendency—the belief that the here and now is all there is.

The only way to counteract this tendency is to intervene most vigorously in the education of those few who come to the university with a strong urge for *un je ne sais quoi*, who fear that they may fail to discover it, and that the cultivation of their

VERNON REGIONAL
JUNIOR COLLEGE LIBRARY

minds is required for the success of their quest. We are long past the age when a whole tradition could be stored up in all students, to be fruitfully used later by some. Only those who are willing to take risks and are ready to believe the implausible are now fit for a bookish adventure. The desire must come from within. People do what they want, and now the most needful things appear so implausible to them that it is hopeless to attempt universal reform. Teachers of writing in state universities, among the noblest and most despised laborers in the academy, have told me that they cannot teach writing to students who do not read, and that it is practically impossible to get them to read, let alone like it. This is where high schools have failed most, filled with teachers who are products of the sixties and reflecting the pallor of university-level humanities. The old teachers who loved Shakespeare or Austen or Donne, and whose only reward for teaching was the perpetuation of their taste, have all but disappeared.

Discarding Wisdom

We have been discarding inherited social and cultural wisdom at an extraordinary rate, a process much accelerated in recent years by the contempt of our fashionable and influential left-wing for all traditional forms. The result is a radical uncivilizing most obvious in the antics of what we have learned to call the underclasses, but apparent in the behavior of all classes of society.

F.W. Brownlow, *Chronicles*, February 1993.

The latest enemy of the vitality of classic texts is feminism. The struggles against elitism and racism in the sixties and seventies had little direct effect on students' relations to books. The democratization of the university helped dismantle its structure and caused it to lose its focus. But the activists had no special quarrel with the classic texts, and they were even a bit infected by their Frankfurt School masters' habit of parading their intimacy with high culture. Radicals had at an earlier stage of egalitarianism already dealt with the monarchic, aristocratic and antidemocratic character of most literary classics by no longer paying attention to their manifest political content. Literary criticism concentrated on the private, the intimate, the feelings, thoughts and relations of individuals, while reducing to the status of a literary convention of the past the fact that the heroes of many classic works were soldiers and statesmen engaged in ruling and faced with political problems. Shakespeare, as he has been read for most of this century, does not constitute a threat

JUNIOR COLLEGE LIBRARY

to egalitarian right thinking. And as for racism, it just did not play a role in the classic literature, at least in the forms in which we are concerned about it today, and no great work of literature is ordinarily considered racist.

But *all* literature up to today is sexist. The Muses never sang to the poets about liberated women. It's the same old *chanson* from the Bible and Homer through Joyce and Proust. And this is particularly grave for literature, since the love interest was most of what remained in the classics after politics was purged in the academy, and was also what drew students to reading them. These books appealed to eros while educating it. So activism has been directed against the content of books. The latest translation of Biblical text—sponsored by the National Council of the Churches of Christ—suppresses gender references to God, so that future generations will not have to grapple with the fact that God was once a sexist. But this technique has only limited applicability. Another tactic is to expunge the most offensive authors—for example, Rousseau—from the education of the young or to include feminist responses in college courses, pointing out the distorting prejudices, and using the books only as evidence of the misunderstanding of woman's nature and the history of injustice to it. Moreover, the great female characters can be used as examples of the various ways women have coped with their enslavement to the sexual role. But never, never, must a student be attracted to those old ways and take them as models for him or herself. However, all this effort is wasted. Students cannot imagine that the old literature could teach them anything about the relations they want to have or will be permitted to have. So they are indifferent.

Having heard over a period of years the same kinds of responses to my question about favorite books, I began to ask students who their heroes are. Again, there is usually silence, and most frequently nothing follows. Why should anyone have heroes? One should be oneself and not form oneself in an alien mold. Here positive ideology supports them: their lack of hero-worship is a sign of maturity. They posit their own values. . . .

Self-Guidance

In America we have only the bourgeoisie, and the love of the heroic is one of the few counterpoises available to us. In us the contempt for the heroic is only an extension of the perversion of the democratic principle that denies greatness and wants everyone to feel comfortable in his skin without having to suffer unpleasant comparisons. Students have not the slightest notion of what an achievement it is to free oneself from public guidance and find resources for guidance within oneself. From what source within themselves would they draw the goals they think they set for themselves? Liberation from the heroic only means that they have no resource whatsoever against conformity to the current "role models." They are constantly thinking of themselves in terms of fixed standards that they did not make. Instead of being overwhelmed by Cyrus, Theseus, Moses or Romulus, they unconsciously act out the roles of the doctors, lawyers, businessmen or TV personalities around them. One can only pity young people without admirations they can respect or avow, who are artificially restrained from the enthusiasm for great virtue.

In encouraging this deformity, democratic relativism joins a branch of conservatism that is impressed by the dangerous political consequences of idealism. These conservatives want young people to know that this tawdry old world cannot respond to their demands for perfection. In the choice between the somewhat arbitrarily distinguished realism and idealism, a sensible person would want to be both, or neither. But, momentarily accepting a distinction I reject, idealism as it is commonly conceived should have primacy in an education, for man is a being who must take his orientation by his possible perfection. To attempt to suppress this most natural of all inclinations because of possible abuses is, almost literally, to throw out the baby with the bath. Utopianism is, as Plato taught us at the outset, the fire with which we must play because it is the only way we can find out what we are. We need to criticize false understandings of Utopia, but the easy way out provided by realism is deadly. As it now stands, students have powerful images of what a perfect body is and pursue it incessantly. But deprived of literary guidance, they no longer have any image of a perfect soul, and hence do not long to have one. They do not even imagine that there is such a thing.

"There is a whole army of [traditionalists] spread out across the country who are boring students into illiteracy, all because they're . . . interested in some kind of quixotic struggle in the name of . . . tradition."

An Emphasis on Western Civilization Is Outdated

Ishmael Reed

Ishmael Reed grew up in the working-class neighborhoods of Buffalo, New York. He is a poet, novelist, and essayist, as well as the founder of the Before Columbus Foundation in Oakland, California. In the following viewpoint, he considers the consequences of illiteracy in America, and places a part of the blame on the prevalence of "monoculturalism"—reading and valuing only the classics of white European civilization. Reed contends that the only way to overcome illiteracy is by relating literature to the reality of America's modern, multicultural society.

As you read, consider the following questions:

1. What, in Reed's view, are some of the consequences of illiteracy?
2. Does Reed acknowledge that the European classics have any value?

Reprinted with the permission of Atheneum Publishers, an imprint of Macmillan Publishing Company, from *Writin' Is Fightin'* by Ishmael Reed. Originally published in the *San Francisco Examiner*, November 1987. Copyright © 1987 by Ishmael Reed.

I'm beginning to believe that Killer Illiteracy ought to rank near heart disease and cancer as one of the leading causes of death among Americans. What you don't know can indeed hurt you, and so those who can neither read nor write lead miserable lives, like Richard Wright's character, Bigger Thomas, born dead with no past or future. If they're hungry they don't know how to fill out an application for food stamps or, since much of the information about the world is shut off from them, may never have heard of the food stamp program. If they're injecting themselves with heroin, the favorite pastime of thousands of people in Northern California who have no better way to stimulate their imaginations, they don't know that dirty needles can give you AIDS, thereby threatening generations of the unborn with their ignorance.

If you're illiterate, people can do anything they want to you. Take your house through equity scams, cheat you, lie to you, bunko you, take your money, even take your life. Illiterate people get used in diabolical experiments such as the Tuskegee Program, in which unsuspecting black males were injected with syphilis by government Dr. Mengeles.

Shoveled Under by Illiteracy

As you go through life X-ing documents, unable to defend yourself against forces hostile to you, people can deprive you of your voting rights through gerrymandering schemes, build a freeway next to your apartment building, or open a retail crack operation on your block, with people coming and going as though you lived next door to Burger King—because you're not articulate enough to fight back, because you don't have sense enough to know what is happening to you, and so you're shoveled under at each turn in your life; you might as well be dead.

One of the joys of reading is the ability to plug into the shared wisdom of mankind. One of my favorite passages from the Bible is "Come, and let us reason together"—Isaiah 1:18. Being illiterate means that you often resort to violence, during the most trivial dispute—the kind of disputes that would inspire hilarious skits on "Saturday Night Live" if they weren't so tragic—because you don't have the verbal skills to talk things out. I'm sure this is the reason why some "minority" males are participating in a mutual extermination to such an extent that the homicide statistics in "minority communities" read as though an Iran-Iraq war of fratricide was happening within our borders.

I'm also convinced that illiteracy is a factor contributing to suicide becoming one of the leading causes of death among white middle-class youngsters, who allow their souls to atrophy from the steady diet of spiritual Wonder Bread: bad music, and bad film, and the outrageous cheapness of superficial culture. When was the last time you saw a movie or TV program that was as good as the best book you've read, and I don't mean what imitation elitists call the classics. I'd settle for Truman Capote, John A. Williams, Cecil Brown, Lawson Inada, Paule Marshall, Xam Wilson Cartier, Victor Cruz, Howard Nemerov, William Kennedy, Paula Gunn Allen, Margaret Atwood, Diane Johnson, Edward Field, Frank Chin, Rudolfo Anaya, Wesley Brown, Lucille Clifton, Al Young, Amiri Baraka, Simon Ortiz, Bob Callahan, Richard Grossinger, David Meltzer, Anna Castillo, Joyce Carol Thomas and Harryette Mullen, a group of writers as good as any you'd find anywhere, but who seldom make the curriculum of oil-money intellectuals like Allan Bloom, author of *The Closing of the American Mind*.

Bloom's love of the classics was revealed as phony by Martha Nussbaum in a devastating piece on this cultural Col. Blimp in the November 5 issue of the *New York Review of Books*. Bloom represents the kind of people who are driving students away from reading. The kind of people who fill our students with dead diction and archaic styles and perpetuate the idea that good writing can be found only in a seventeenth-century vault.

Illiteracy not only affects members of the "underclass" but reaches into the centers of higher education. It has been revealed that many of our college students have difficulty with even the bonehead level of English. To remedy this situation, AWP newsletter, a publication of the associated writing program, is urging that more professional writers, a sort of United States Writing Corps, be sent into our public schools and universities to acquaint students with writing as a useful tool, as well as something that enriches one's experience.

To say that the job should be left exclusively to critics and theorists is to say that a food critic knows as much about food as a chef, or that one can learn to build a cabinet by reading the history of furniture. AWP is also correct in its proposal that the hiring, rank and tenure of teachers of writing "should be based on the quality of the individual's writing and teaching" and that "academic degrees should not be considered a requirement or a major criterion which would overrule the importance of the writer's achievement in the art." This proposal becomes more important when you learn that a poet of Philip Levine's stature was denied a teaching job at a local university because he lacked a Ph.D. These people who fill the curriculum with thousands of courses on Shakespeare would have denied Shakespeare a job because he lacked a degree.

One of the exercises I give when I visit Berkeley and Oakland schools involves having students write about their activities, from the time they rose in the morning until they arrived in school. This exercise not only gives me an opportunity to demonstrate how raw material, through skillful editing and revi-

25

sion, can be transformed into a polished manuscript, but how writing can involve normal conversational language, and that the techniques of fiction and poetry can be found in everyday language, and that writing can be fun, and not just a solemn visit to the cemetery, the opinion of the great mind who included in the Oakland high school equivalency test a question that only a specialist in middle English should be required to answer.

The person who designed this question perhaps thinks of himself as a traditionalist, who, like many traditionalists, desires to impose bigotry upon the "ancients," who were a cosmopolitan people, and would never put themselves in dumb antiintellectual positions like opposing ethnic or women's studies, or bilingual education, or trying to avoid linguistic change by making one language the official language of the state, a gesture as foolish as opposing a comet. How many of these traditionalists will admit that Terence, a Roman playwright, was black, or that a few of the early popes were black, or that if it weren't for Arab translators, they wouldn't even have access to the Great Books they're always pretending to love?

Embracing Differences Among Us

By perpetuating the rhetoric of separatism—"us" versus "them," all versus nothing—and by accentuating rather than embracing a difference, detractors of multiculturalism create a self-fulfilling prophecy of polarization that subverts attempts at unity. . . . After all, we are only as strong as the weakest among us; by appropriately and adequately securing each of our diverse components, we fortify the integrity of our shared American heritage.

Brenda Mitchell-Powell, *MultiCultural Review*, October 1992.

Left up to these geniuses we'd all be speaking Old Norse. There is a whole army of these types spread out across the country who are boring students into illiteracy, all because they're more interested in some kind of quixotic struggle in the name of a mythical tradition instead of being concerned about whether our students can read and write.

I studied, and enjoyed, white male literature for about the first 20 years of my life (the few women we read were tokens, like the Brontë sisters), but I really became interested in writing when I read James Baldwin and Richard Wright. They proved to me that a person of my background could write as well as the rest of them. You'd think that the modern curriculum would include books by Hispanics, Asian Americans, Afro-Americans— not just the token one or two who are there for the wrong reasons—so as to demonstrate to children of those cultures what persons of their backgrounds have accomplished.

Including multicultural literature in the curriculum would also acquaint students who are ignorant of other American cultures with the range of experience found within them. Certainly, if, according to Terry Eagleton, the turn-of-the-century goal of teaching literature was to create better men, then literature can also be used to promote understanding between groups, a job that's unfortunately left to TV and the movies, whose goal seems to be that of raising lynch mobs against minorities. I knew that my course in multicultural literature at Dartmouth was a success when a black student told me that after reading John Okada and Louis Chou, she'd discovered that Asian Americans weren't all the same, a lesson that our hysterical inflammatory news media, which are always lumping thirty-eight culturally distinct groups as one people, haven't learned.

Certainly, the monoculturalists and their allies who have such a powerful influence over the design of the school curricula must share some of the blame for the appalling rate of literacy in the United States, but parents who leave the job of teaching writing and reading to the schools must also bear some of the responsibility.

These parents don't have a book in the house, not even a newspaper that can be as instructive as any work of literature, because some of our finest writers have been newspaper people. James Reston, Robert Maynard, Brenda Payton, Warren Hinckle, Hunter Thompson are as good as any of the "major" writers now publishing in the United States. For parents to believe that the job should be left to teachers means that they haven't visited a classroom where one teacher is in charge of thirty students, and because of budget cuts lacks resources, and must behave as policeman for a generation of surly anarchists who don't receive any discipline at home. These parents don't attend PTA meetings so that they might understand what teachers and schools are up against in a time of greed, or what the stock market calls excessive consumption, when the country club set in Washington is willing to sacrifice the younger generation as long as they're getting theirs; but ultimately, there is no excuse for literate parents not helping with the tutoring of their children. . . .

And for those misled children who keep us up half the night with their squealing around the corners on bald tires and indulging in other silly expressions of manhood, and who think that literature is silly, I have a story to recount. An editor from *Playboy* called to ask about a passage from a Christmas novel I wrote titled *The Terrible Twos*. She said they were running an interview with an athlete and he'd quoted from it. His name: Kareem Abdul-Jabbar.

"The historical records from each era . . . form a choir of resounding voices affirming Christianity to be the base of our nation."

Christian Principles Should Guide American Government

David Barton

Christian television frequently features David Barton, who forcefully defends the view that America developed as a Christian society and nation. Barton observes that the phrase "separation of church and state" does not actually appear in the Constitution, and he documents a number of important court cases that suggest the legal prominence of Christianity, especially in the nineteenth century. Barton has a degree in Religious Education from Oral Roberts University, and is the author of *America: To Pray or Not to Pray* and *What Happened in Education*, as well as *The Myth of Separation*, from which the following viewpoint is excerpted.

As you read, consider the following questions:

1. Why does Barton emphasize the Holy Trinity case, and Justice Brewer's opinion at that time?
2. How does Barton define "organic utterances"?
3. Why does the author say that state courts can be more authoritative than federal courts?

From *The Myth of Separation* by David Barton. 5th edition. Copyright 1992 by David Barton. Wallbuilders Press, Aledo, TX 76008. Used by permission.

Is there nothing to document the intent of the Founders? It would be logical that any rulings made by the courts in the years immediately following the framing of the Constitution would accurately reflect the Founders' intent. Are those early accounts still available? Fortunately, they are. This viewpoint will examine several of those rulings, some dating back to 1795. In many of these cases, justices on the courts had personally participated in drafting and ratifying the Constitution. When ruling on a case, they did not have to struggle with intent—they knew their own intentions! . . .

Our Founders would *never* have tolerated the separation of church and state as it now exists. Only in a nightmare could the Founders have envisioned what the Court is now doing with the First Amendment!

Church of the Holy Trinity v. United States, 1892

This case provides a good starting point, for it cites several of the earlier cases. This case centered on an 1885 federal law concerning immigration which declared:

> It shall be unlawful for any person, company, partnership, or corporation, in any manner whatsoever . . . to in any way assist or encourage the importation . . . of any alien or . . . foreigners, into the United States . . . under contract or agreement . . . to perform labor or service of any kind.

Two years later, in 1887, the Church of the Holy Trinity in New York employed a clergyman from England as its pastor. That employment was challenged by the United States Attorney General's office as a violation of the law. The case eventually reached the Supreme Court.

The first half of the Court's decision dealt with what it termed "absurd" application of laws. The Court was not saying that the legislation was absurd, for in the early years the Court rarely criticized the legislature since it was the voice of the people. "Absurd" referred to cases where an interpretation by the letter of the law and not by the spirit or intent of its framers would lead to absurd results.

The Court examined the Congressional records of the hearings surrounding this legislation and established, from the legislators' own testimony, that the law was enacted solely to preclude an influx of cheap and unskilled labor for work on the railroads. Although the church's alleged violation was certainly within the letter of the law, it was not within its spirit. The Court concluded that only an "absurd" application of the Constitution would allow a restriction on Christianity:

> No purpose of action against religion can be imputed to any legislation, state or national, because this is a religious people. . . . This is a Christian nation.

The Court resolved the legal question within the first half of its written ruling and devoted the remainder to establishing that this nation is indeed Christian and why it would be constitutionally "absurd" and legally impossible to legislate any restrictions on Christianity. Despite the Court's use of only brief historical quotations, its references comprised eight of the sixteen pages in the decision. Justice Brewer, who delivered the opinion of the Court, gave the basis for the Court's conclusion:

> This is a religious people. This is historically true. From the discovery of this continent to the present hour, there is a single voice making this affirmation. The commission to Christopher Columbus . . . [recited] that "it is hoped that by God's assistance some of the continents and islands in the ocean will be discovered. . . ." The first colonial grant made to Sir Walter Raleigh in 1584 . . . and the grant authorizing him to enact statutes for the government of the proposed colony provided that "they be not against the true Christian faith. . . ." The first charter of Virginia, granted by King James I in 1606 . . . commenced the grant in these words: ". . . in propagating of Christian Religion to such People as yet live in Darkness. . . ."

> Language of similar import may be found in the subsequent charters of that colony . . . in 1609 and 1611; and the same is true of the various charters granted to the other colonies. In language more or less emphatic is the establishment of the Christian religion declared to be one of the purposes of the grant. The celebrated compact made by the Pilgrims in the Mayflower, 1620, recites: "Having undertaken for the Glory of God, and advancement of the Christian faith . . . a voyage to plant the first colony in the northern parts of Virginia. . . ."

> The fundamental orders of Connecticut, under which a provisional government was instituted in 1638-1639, commence with this declaration: ". . . And well knowing where a people are gathered together the word of God requires that to maintain the peace and union . . . there should be an orderly and decent government established according to God . . . to maintain and preserve the liberty and purity of the gospel of our Lord Jesus which we now profess . . . of the said gospel [which] is now practiced amongst us."

> In the charter of privileges granted by William Penn to the province of Pennsylvania, in 1701, it is recited: ". . . no people can be truly happy, though under the greatest enjoyment of civil liberties, if abridged of . . . their religious profession and worship. . . ."

> Coming nearer to the present time, the Declaration of Independence recognizes the presence of the Divine in human affairs in these words: "We hold these truths to be self-evident, that all men are created equal, that they are endowed by their Creator with certain unalienable Rights . . ."; ". . . appealing to the Supreme Judge of the world for the rectitude of our inten-

tions . . ."; "And for the support of this Declaration, with a firm reliance on the Protection of Divine Providence, we mutually pledge to each other our Lives, our Fortunes, and our sacred Honor."

The Court continued with example after example, citing portions from the forty-four state constitutions (the number of states in 1892). The Court's historical discourse continued for several pages until finally summarizing its findings:

There is no dissonance in these declarations. There is a universal language pervading them all, having one meaning; they affirm and reaffirm that this is a religious nation. These are not individual sayings, declarations of private persons: they are organic utterances; they speak the voice of the entire people. While because of a general recognition of this truth the question has seldom been presented to the courts, yet we find that in *Updegraph* v. *The Commonwealth*, it was decided that, "Christianity, general Christianity, is, and always has been, a part of the common law . . . not Christianity with an established church . . . but Christianity with liberty of conscience to all men." And in *The People* v. *Ruggles*, Chancellor Kent, the great commentator on American law, speaking as Chief Justice of the Supreme Court of New York, said: "The people of this State, in common with the people of this country, profess the general doctrines of Christianity, as the rule of their faith and practice. . . . We are a Christian people, and the morality of the country is deeply engrafted upon Christianity, and not upon the doctrines or worship of those impostors [other religions]." And in the famous case of *Vidal* v. *Girard's Executors*, this Court . . . observed: "It is also said, and truly, that the Christian religion is a part of the common law. . . ." These, and many other matters which might be noticed, add a volume of unofficial declarations to the mass of organic utterances that this is a Christian nation.

This stands as quite a convincing and broad-based argument! The Court quoted directly from eighteen sources, alluded to over forty others, and acknowledged "many other" and "a volume" more from which selections could have been made.

The Court cited *People* v. *Ruggles*, *Updegraph* v. *Commonwealth*, and *Vidal* v. *Girard's Executors* in establishing its conclusion. The *Ruggles* case was decided by the Supreme Court of New York in 1811, *Updegraph* by the Supreme Court of Pennsylvania in 1826, and *Vidal* by the United States Supreme Court in 1844. . . .

Currently, the federal Supreme Court is very high profile and affects national and private life through its far-reaching decisions. Consequently, a state's supreme court is now perceived as a less credible source than the federal Supreme Court. However, this was not the attitude of earlier years. For 150 years after the ratification of the Constitution, the states were considered the highest source of authority. Most disputes went no higher than state courts, and only unusual circumstances would cause a case to go to the federal Supreme Court (i.e., disputes between states, cases involving federal territories not yet states, cases not involving a jury decision, etc.).

Therefore, on items concerning religion and Christianity, the federal courts were considered *less* of an authority than the state courts. As the Court itself had noted in the *Holy Trinity* case, it had few occasions in which to decide on issues affecting Christianity:

> While because of a general recognition of this truth [that we are a Christian nation], the question has seldom been presented to the courts.

When the federal Court did render a decision touching Christianity, it frequently cited the decisions of the state supreme courts, as it did in *Holy Trinity*. . . .

Other "Organic Utterances"

In *Church of the Holy Trinity* v. *United States*, 1892, the Court explained that it was the "organic utterances" which proved that this was a Christian nation. "Organic," in a legal sense, simply means "belonging to the fundamental or constitutional law" and can be comprised of both historical information and of previous legal rulings based on such historical information. "Organic utterances" are the base on which laws are built and are therefore part of the law—they are what judges term the "common law." The Court noted that the "mass of organic utterances" provided "a volume of unofficial declarations," prompting their official conclusion that "this is a Christian nation."

The Founders' Faith in God

The fathers of this nation never dreamed that separation of church and state meant that God should be separated from government. The government buildings in Washington bear ample testimony to the belief that faith in God is the basis for establishing laws and running the affairs of a nation. For example, the Ten Commandments hang over the head of the chief justice of the Supreme Court. . . . In the rotunda the words "In God We Trust" are engraved, and on the Library of Congress we have "The heavens declare the glory of God and the firmament showeth His handiwork." The Washington monument and other government buildings contain phrases of Scripture.

Erwin J. Lutzer, *Exploding the Myths That Could Destroy America*, 1986.

The quantity of organic utterances (historical material) available for proving that this is a Christian nation are such that one might be tempted to say, as did the Apostle John when writing about Jesus, that if everything "were written down, I suppose that even the whole world would not have room for the books that would be written" (John 21:25). Even though this viewpoint is filled with numerous selections typical of the mass, they still only "skim the surface" of that which is available. The reader can become his own investigator of history and quickly discover how much more could be added to that which is presented here.

The following selections are presented in the same chronological order utilized by the Court: "from the discovery of the continent to the present hour." The historical records from each era, when combined together in this viewpoint, indeed form a choir of resounding voices affirming Christianity to be the base of our nation, government, and educational system. The reader will soon be convinced of what the Supreme Court declared: "this is a Christian nation.". . .

America's First Colonies

Following Columbus' discovery of the western lands, other explorers ventured onto the new continent, making property claims for their own nations. Soon, groups of prospective colonists began to approach their sovereign and request land charters in the new nation. In 1606, a charter was obtained from King James I for a permanent settlement in the new world in Virginia. That charter reveals the colonists' declared reasons for traveling to the new world:

> To make Habitation . . . and to deduce a Colony of sundry of our People into that Part of America, commonly called Virginia . . . in propagating of Christian religion to such People as yet live in Darkness . . . [to] bring . . . a settled and quiet Government.

In 1609, another charter was granted for Virginia:

> Because the principal Effect which we can desire or expect of this Action is the Conversion . . . of the people in those parts unto the true Worship of God and the Christian Religion.

The Pilgrims arrived in America on the Mayflower in November of 1620. Before disembarking, they drafted and signed the Mayflower Compact, the first plan of government formed solely in America. That government compact was brief and concise, proclaiming their purpose for coming to America and affirming their commitment to that purpose:

> Having undertaken for the Glory of God, and Advancement of the Christian Faith . . . a Voyage to plant the first colony in the northern Parts of Virginia . . . [we] combine ourselves together into a civil Body Politick, for . . . Furtherance of the Ends aforesaid.

The First Charter of Massachusetts, dated March 1629, reflected similar goals. It was granted so that:

33

> Our said people . . . maie be soe religiously, peaceablie, and
> civilly governed, as their good life and orderlie conversation
> maie wynn and incite the natives of [that] country to the
> knowledg and obedience of the onlie true God and Savior of
> mankinde, and the Christian fayth, which, in our royal inten-
> tion, is . . . the principall ende of this plantation.

The Puritans arrived nearly a decade after the Pilgrims. During their journey to America, their leader, John Winthrop, authored a work which described their intended role in America—
A Model of Christian Charity:

> Wee are a Company professing our selues fellow members of
> Christ . . . knitt together by this bond of loue. . . . Wee are en-
> tered into Covenant with him for this worke.

Winthrop warned that since they were declaring to the world
that they were witnesses of the Christian lifestyle, there was an
awesome responsibility resting upon them:

> For wee must Consider that wee shall be as a Citty vpon a
> Hill, the eies of all people are vppon vs; soe that if wee shall
> deale falsely with our god in this worke wee haue vndertaken
> and soe cause him to withdrawe his present help from vs, wee
> shall be made a story and a by-word through the world. . . .

As the number of colonists and settlements increased, so did
the need for government. Even though each colony relied heavily on the personal self-control and integrity of its individual
members, the colonists recognized the benefit of civil regulations. They thus produced the first constitution ever written in
the United States: the Fundamental Orders of Connecticut. This
constitution, written primarily by Puritan minister Thomas
Hooker, was the beginning of American government. According
to historians, our own federal Constitution is "in lineal descent
more nearly related to that of Connecticut than to that of any of
the other thirteen colonies." The charge delivered to the committee which convened to frame these laws was to make them:
"As near the law of God as they can be."

On January 14, 1639, the men from Hartford, Wethersfield,
and Windsor gathered in Hartford and adopted this new constitution. Its preamble proclaimed their reason for establishing this
government:

> Well knowing when a people are gathered together the word
> of God requires, that to meinteine the peace and union of
> such a people, there should bee an orderly and decent gov-
> ernement established according to God.

It further explained how this was to be attained:

> Enter into combination and confederation together, to mein-
> teine and preserve the libberty and purity of the gospell of our
> Lord Jesus which we now profess. . . . Which, according to the
> truth of the said Gospell, is now practised amongst us; as
> also, in our civill affaires to be guided and governed accord-

ing to such lawes, rules, orders, and decrees.

When the colonists of Exeter, New Hampshire, established their government seven months later, they expressed the same rationale:

> Considering with ourselves the holy will of God and our own necessity, that we should not live without wholesome laws and civil government among us, of which we are altogether destitute, do, in the name of Christ and in the sight of God, combine ourselves together to erect and set up among us such government as shall be, to our best discerning, agreeable to the will of God.

A similar proclamation was made when Massachusetts, Connecticut, New Plymouth, and New Haven formed the New England Confederation in 1643:

> We all came into these parts of America, with one and the same end and aim, namely, to advance the Kingdom of our Lord Jesus Christ.

In 1644, the New Haven Colony adopted rules for their courts:

> The judicial laws of God as they were delivered by Moses . . . [are to] be a rule to all the courts in this jurisdiction.

In 1669, the Fundamental Constitutions of Carolina was drawn up by John Locke. It required people to: (1) believe that there is a God, (2) in court, recognize Divine justice and human responsibility, and (3) be a church member in order to be a freeman of the colony.

Christian Officials Would Enhance Morality

It is a high principle of statesmanship that the execution of a sovereign purpose be intrusted to hands in sympathy with it. A righteous purpose in the nation would call righteous men to office. The State, truly Christian, would not intrust the administration of government to the enemies of God and of religion. . . . That is not a Christian nation in which a preponderating Christian population *might*, but that in which it *does* control the national life.

The Christian Statesman, September 2, 1867.

In 1665 the New York legislature passed an act to uphold "the public worship of God" and instruction of "the people in the true religion."

In 1681, the Quaker minister William Penn received a land grant giving him the land between New York and Maryland, the area later called Pennsylvania. On receiving this new land, Penn, in a letter on January 1, 1681, professed:

God that has given it me . . . will, I believe, bless and make it the seed of a nation.

The following year, Penn wrote the Frame of Government for this new territory. It was to:

Make and establish such laws as shall best preserve true Christian and civil liberty, in all opposition to all unchristian . . . practices.

The laws were very simple—whatever was Christian was legal, whatever was not Christian was illegal. Penn also told the Russian Czar, Peter the Great, that:

"If thou wouldst rule well, thou must rule for God, and to do that, thou must be ruled by him." Penn also said that "those who will not be governed by God will be ruled by tyrants."

An article on Penn that appeared in the 1819 London *Biographical Review* stated that he:

Established an absolute toleration; it was his wish that every man who believed in God should partake of the rights of a citizen; and that every man who adored Him as a Christian, of whatever sect he might be, should be a partaker in authority.

The differentiation was clear: anyone who believed in God could be a citizen, but only Christians could be part of the civil authority. The "absolute toleration" was reflected in the inclusion of Christians in government "of whatever sect they might be." As with so many of the Founders, Penn felt the issue was not whether an individual was from the proper denomination, but whether he was Christian.

In 1697, the New Jersey governor made a proclamation "in obedience to the laws of God" which enacted statutes "encouraging of religion and virtue, particularly the observance of the Lord's day." The influence of Christianity and the Bible on New Jersey is seen even in the inscription that appeared on the 1665 seal of the East Jersey Colony: Proverbs 14:34—"Righteousness exalteth a nation."

Christianity was the essential ingredient in the early growth and orderly development of the new world in its colonization, government, and education. Virtually every significant achievement of our early years was accomplished under the influence of Christianity.

"The Christian nation concept has never been embraced by the Supreme Court as officially binding judicial policy."

Christian Principles Should Not Guide American Government

Rob Boston

In the following viewpoint, Rob Boston reviews the historical background of the claim that the United States is a Christian nation. He discusses relevant court cases, noting that state courts of the nineteenth century often contradicted the plain language of the Constitution, which in Boston's view is founded on the concept of the separation of church and state. Boston is an assistant editor of the journal *Church and State*.

As you read, consider the following questions:

1. In Boston's opinion, what does the Constitution say about God, Jesus Christ, and Christianity?
2. How do Justice Brewer's later views contradict his opinion in the *Holy Trinity* case?
3. What happened to the nineteenth-century movement to amend the Constitution to formally make the United States a Christian nation?

Rob Boston, "Is America a 'Christian Nation'?" Reprinted with permission from the January 1993 issue of *Church & State*, the monthly magazine of Americans United for Separation of Church and State.

The concept of America as a "Christian nation" has been with the country since its origins. Most often, the term has sparked controversy and ill will because it has been used to elevate the role of one faith over others and to further the politics of exclusion on the basis of religious belief. This explains why so many Americans are offended when public officials use the term today.

The idea that the United States should be officially Christian was explicitly rejected by James Madison and the other framers of the Constitution. Instead, they provided for a system of separation of church and state that guarantees religious freedom for all individuals and groups—Christian and non-Christian alike.

Nevertheless, the concept of America as a Christian society has been strongly advocated by religious conservatives since the colonial period, and the movement reoccurs frequently in history. Over the years, even some judges and assorted government officials have expressed sympathy for that viewpoint.

To the modern-day Religious Right, these assertions are proof that the United States is, or once was, officially a "Christian nation." Most constitutional scholars believe otherwise. They point out that the Constitution contains no references to God, Jesus Christ or Christianity—a deliberate move on the part of the framers who thought government should be given no power to intrude into religious matters. (During the debates surrounding the drafting and ratification of the Constitution, a minority faction argued for some sort of official recognition of Christianity, but its views were rejected.) Had a Christian nation been the intent of the framers, historians point out, the concept would have been featured prominently in the Constitution.

The Rejection of the Christian Nation Concept

Many Religious Right boosters are also unaware that officials of the early U.S. government on at least one occasion formally declared that the United States was not founded on the Christian faith. The Treaty of Tripoli, a trade agreement signed between the United States and the Muslim region of North Africa in 1797, bluntly states that "the Government of the United States is not, in any sense, founded on the Christian religion."

The language was inserted into the document by trade negotiator Joel Barlow. The Senate approved the agreement indicating that they saw the provision as non-controversial and in line with the character of the new nation's government. (The treaty was signed by John Adams, the second president, and the provision cited above remained in it for eight years until the agreement was renegotiated.)

Unable to find much support for the "Christian nation" concept in post-Revolutionary War America, Religious Right activists look to a different period of history as their model for a

Christian republic—a period that began before the Civil War and extended well into the 20th century.

Church-state matters during these decades were left chiefly to state legislators, and disputes, if they occurred at all, were usually resolved by state courts. Judges at this level were often appointed through political patronage systems. As a result, decisions sometimes emerged that today are seen as at odds with religious freedom and separation of church and state.

Many state courts in the 19th century did refer to the United States as a "Christian nation" or implied that Christianity should receive some type of special favor from the state. James Kent, a New York Supreme Court justice, declared in an 1811 blasphemy case, "[T]he people of this state, in common with the people of this country, profess the general principles of Christianity as the rule of their faith and practice; and to scandalize the author of these doctrines is not only in a religious point of view, extremely impious, but even in respect to the obligations due to society, is a gross violation of decency and good order."

The Trinity Church Case

The U.S. Supreme Court even fell victim to this "Christian nation" mentality on one occasion. Religious Right activists frequently cite 1892's *Holy Trinity Church v. United States* decision as proof that the high court considered the United States to have a religious foundation. However, they usually do not tell the whole story.

In the ruling, Justice David Brewer flatly declared "this is a Christian nation." To this day, historians debate what Brewer meant by the term. It is unclear whether he meant to say the country's laws should reflect Christian moral principles or was simply acknowledging the fact that most Americans are Christians and that Christianity has played a prominent role in American life.

A strong argument can be made for the latter proposition by examining a case that came along five years after the *Holy Trinity* ruling. The dispute centered on legalized prostitution in New Orleans. A Methodist congregation challenged a city ordinance allowing prostitution in one area of the city. The church argued that prostitution should be illegal everywhere in New Orleans, insisting that the activity is inconsistent with Christianity "which the Supreme Court of the United States says is the foundation of our government. . . ."

Writing for a unanimous court, Brewer completely ignored the congregation's argument and upheld the New Orleans policy. Brewer's bypass suggests that he did not mean to imply in *Holy Trinity* that the United States should enforce the dictates of Christianity by law. Had that been the justice's intention, he surely would have upheld the Methodists' claim.

Possibly because his phrase was being taken out of context, Brewer felt compelled to explain his views in greater detail. In 1905 he published a short book titled *The United States A Christian Nation*. In that volume Brewer elaborates on what he meant in the famous *Holy Trinity* passage.

Judge, © 1992, Kansas City Star. Reprinted with permission.

"But in what sense can [the United States] be called a Christian nation?" asked Brewer. "Not in the sense that Christianity is the established religion or the people are compelled in any manner to support it. On the contrary, the Constitution specifically provides that 'Congress shall make no law respecting an establishment of religion or prohibiting the free exercise thereof.' Neither is it Christian in the sense that all its citizens are either in fact or in name Christians. On the contrary, all religions have free scope within its borders. Numbers of our people profess other religions, and many reject all."

Continued Brewer, "Nor is it Christian in the sense that a profession of Christianity is a condition of holding office or otherwise engaging in public service, or essential to recognition either politically or socially. In fact, the government as a legal organization is independent of all religions."

The passage strongly suggests that Brewer simply meant that the United States is "Christian" in the sense that many of its people belong to Christian denominations and many of the country's customs and traditions have roots in Christianity. Brewer expounds on this theme for the rest of his 98-page book, predicting that Christianity will one day unify the American masses and make the United States a leader in world affairs.

Whatever Brewer's intent, it is important to realize that the Christian nation concept has never been embraced by the Supreme Court as officially binding judicial policy. The *Holy Trinity* ruling, for example, is a legal anomaly that has been cited as precedent only once by the Supreme Court since it was handed down.

It is also important to note that not all 19th-century courts saw the American government as religiously grounded. As early as the 1840s, judges began questioning the legal basis for the doctrine. In 1872, the Ohio Supreme Court expressly rejected a claim grounded on the Christian nation concept. "Those who make this assertion [that America is a Christian nation] can hardly be serious, and intend the real import of their language," the court wrote. "If Christianity is a *law* of the State, like every other law, it must have a *sanction*. . . . No one seriously contends for any such doctrine in this country, or I might say, in this age of the world."

The Religious Right

With judicial rulings falling on both sides of the issue, 19th-century precursors to today's Religious Right organizations sought to promote the Christian nation concept by securing passage of a constitutional amendment that would grant official endorsement to Christianity.

The movement was spearheaded by the National Reform Association (NRA), a coalition formed in 1863 by representatives from 11 Protestant denominations. One of the group's stated goals was "to secure such an amendment to the Constitution of the United States as will declare the nation's allegiance to Jesus Christ and its acceptance of the moral laws of the Christian religion, and so indicate that this is a Christian nation. . . ."

In 1864 the group petitioned Congress to amend the preamble of the Constitution, adding a section "humbly acknowledging Almighty God as the source of all authority and power in civil government, the Lord Jesus Christ as the Ruler among the nations, His revealed will as the supreme law of the land, in order to constitute a Christian government."

Critics charge that the "Christian amendment" was clearly designed to be the first step in a broader NRA agenda. The group also advocated strict enforcement of blasphemy and Sabbath laws, religious tests for public officeholders, limits on divorce, and an increase in the religious content in the nation's public schools.

Religion Must Not Guide Government

Fasting and prayer are religious exercises; the enjoying of them is an act of religious discipline. . . . Civil powers alone have been given to the President of the United States, and he has no authority to direct the religious exercises of his constituents.

Thomas Jefferson, on declining to officially proclaim Thanksgiving Day.

"The Christian nation concept has a less than savory reputation among historians," notes AU Legal Counsel Steven Green, who is writing a doctoral dissertation on the concept. "'Christian nation' was a code word for an evangelical socio-religious perspective and was used to marginalize all religious nonconformists. Throughout the 19th century prosecutors and judges applied the concept to justify Sabbath and other sumptuary laws that excluded Jews, Catholics, Adventists and freethinkers from the political process."

The NRA's Christian nation amendment languished in Congress for years, occasionally being reintroduced in different versions. Finally in 1874 the House Judiciary Committee voted against its adoption. The congressional panel said it took the action "in full realization of the dangers which the union between church and state had imposed upon so many nations of the Old World, with great unanimity that it was inexpedient to put anything into the Constitution or frame of government which might be construed to be a reference to any religious creed or doctrine.". . .

Generally speaking, when Religious Right leaders use the term "Christian nation," they are referring to their desire to see the nation's laws reflect the narrow sectarian principles they themselves hold—not simply saying that most Americans identify with Christian denominations. These misguided activists want to send a signal that only those individuals with the "correct" religious views are real Americans.

Mainstream American religious denominations do not use the term "Christian nation" or speak of such a concept as desirable, recognizing that it offends and excludes those Americans who are not affiliated with the Christian faith. Thus, the term is closely tied to the Religious Right and its extreme religiopolitical goals. Today, as in previous eras of American life, it is unmistakably a term of exclusion, not inclusion.

"The Puritan way . . . may well contain the beginnings of answers to our own family problems."

The Principles of Puritanism Would Be a Constructive Influence

Peter Marshall and David Manuel

From childhood, most of us have an image of the Puritans fixed in our minds. After braving the sea in a difficult ocean voyage, they land in Massachusetts, where, with the help of the Indians, they overcome terrible hardships and near starvation. Partly as a result of Nathaniel Hawthorne's influential masterpiece *The Scarlet Letter*, we also think of the Puritans as stern, humorless and repressive. In the following viewpoint, Peter Marshall and David Manuel argue that this image is largely shallow and stereotypical. They emphasize that the Puritans helped establish a new society in difficult circumstances, and created a positive morality which is much needed yet today. Marshall currently conducts a traveling and speaking ministry across America. Manuel has a B.A. in English from Yale University, and has also authored several books, including *Like a Mighty River* and *The Jesus Factor*.

As you read, consider the following questions:

1. In what ways is the popular image of the Puritan inaccurate? How were the Puritans, according to the authors, more "human"?
2. What values do the authors argue were typical of the Puritan family?

From Peter Marshall and David Manuel, *The Light of Glory*. Copyright 1977 by Peter Marshall and David Manuel. Reprinted by permission of Fleming H. Revell, a division of Baker Book House.

A recent novel by a best-selling author purports to trace the lives of the Winthrop family down through three centuries. The jacket of the book shows people dressed in the garb of different eras, all of them ominously overshadowed by a brooding gray eminence which presumably is the specter of John Winthrop, Senior. A quick look inside confirms that the author has indeed accepted the modern stereotype of the Puritans. Nearly everyone today seems to believe that the Puritans were bluenosed killjoys in tall black hats, a somber group of sin-obsessed, witch-hunting bigots, "whose main occupation was to prevent each other from having any fun and whose sole virtue lay in their furniture."

How could such a monstrous misrepresentation have been so widely and so quickly accepted? For the anti-Puritan phenomenon has arisen largely within the twentieth century. Almost no negative bias can be found among nineteenth-century historians; on the contrary, they gladly gave the Puritans the lion's share of the credit for setting the direction of this nation. Why then, the sudden prejudice in so many hearts?

The answer seems to lie in the fact that not in the three hundred and fifty years of our history has a spirit of rebellion gained such a tight hold on the minds and wills of the American people. What could be more of an anathema to such an attitude than the cheerful submission to authority, holy service, and corporate commitment which the Puritans personified! If there is one people in the history of the country whose example Satan hates more than any other, it is the Puritans. And since rebellion is his specialty, it is no wonder that the Puritans have received such a bad press of late!

Thus, as customs which have been in effect in this country for more than three hundred years are vilified and torn down, the most withering negative epithet one hears attached to them is *puritanical*, be it the work ethic, chastity before marriage, modesty in decorum and apparel, shops closed in observance of the Lord's Day, legislation against immorality. . . . The list is endless, and the traditions are crumbling under an ever more determined onslaught.

We have found these much-maligned Christians to be sinners like ourselves, but also warm and human, and possessed of remarkable spiritual wisdom and discernment.

But, we asked ourselves, what about their legendary self-righteousness and intolerance? Had they not banished Roger Williams, simply because he spoke his mind and because his doctrine did not happen to agree with theirs? The founder of Rhode Island has become the hero of outspoken anti-establishment academics.

And had they not also expelled Anne Hutchinson? She now has a river (and a parkway) named after her. The dilemma we now faced was: If such narrow-minded self-righteousness was an inevitable by-product of man's attempts to establish the Kingdom of God on earth, did that not bring the whole matter of the feasibility of a Bible Commonwealth into question? And if the Puritans *were* attempting the impossible, how much more impossible would it be today?

Taking Sin Seriously

The scarlet letter *A* for *adulteress* which Hester Prynne, the heroine of Nathaniel Hawthorne's famous novel, was forced to wear, seared its way into the psyche of nineteenth-century America. A century later, Arthur Miller's play about the Salem witch-hunters, "The Crucible," carried the popular image of the Puritans further. And countless other modern novelists and dramatists have presented the Puritans as morbidly preoccupied with sin and guilt. Is there any truth to the picture?

There is no question that the Puritans took sin seriously—far more seriously than most American Christians today. But they had good reason: they knew that the very success or failure of God's New Israel hung on their willingness to deal strongly with sin—in themselves first, but also in those who had been called with them to build the Kingdom. Indeed, there could be no compromise where the presence of sin was concerned. For an example of the fruit of compromise, all they needed to do was to look across the Atlantic at what was happening in England. And so they did not shy away from facing up to sin or dealing with it.

There is one modern historian who has consistently exposed the popular negative stereotype of the Puritans for the patently false view that it is. He is the late Perry Miller, widely regarded as the dean of Puritan historians. Almost single-handedly, his works have been responsible for a major revision in the thinking of serious students of American history. (But unfortunately this is only a minute segment of the American public.)

Here is what Miller had to say about the Puritans' attitude towards sin:

> Puritanism would make every man an expert psychologist, to detect all makeshift "rationalizations," to shatter without pity the sweet dreams of self-enhancement in which the ego takes refuge from reality. A large quantity of Puritan sermons were devoted to . . . exposing not merely the conscious duplicity of evil men, but the abysmal tricks which the subconscious can play upon the best of men. The duty of the Puritan in this world was to know himself—without sparing himself one bit, without flattering himself in the slightest, without concealing from himself a single unpleasant fact about himself.

This willingness to look unblinkingly at the worst side of their own natures made them consummate realists. It also was responsible for the extraordinary compassion which became the hallmark of such exceptional leaders among them as John Winthrop, Thomas Hooker, and Cotton Mather. For once you really *knew* how corrupt your own nature was at its core, you would be much more inclined to readily forgive the sinfulness of others.

Puritanism and Values

The orthodox colonies were originally medieval states, based on a fixed will of God, dedicated to the explicitly just, good, and honest. Men were arranged in hierarchical ranks, the lower obedient to the upper, with magistrates and scholars at the top. Things were right or wrong intrinsically, not relatively, so that the price of a piece of cloth could be determined by theologians. . . . The sermons were releases from a sickness of soul which otherwise found no surcease. They were professions of a society that knew it was doing wrong, but could not help itself, because the wrong thing was also the right thing. From such ceremonies men arose with new strength and courage: having acknowledged what was amiss, the populace could go back to their fields and benches and ships, trusting that a covenanted Jehovah would remember his bond.

Perry Miller, *The New England Mind*, 1953.

Anyone who searches the church records will find that Puritan discipline, although strict by necessity, was almost always tempered with great mercy. The reason it was strict (and enforced by civil law), was that they all felt that the entire fabric of their covenant life together depended on living in proper order and in joint obedience to the laws of God. Thus when one sinned, it affected them all. Tryal Pore, a young girl arraigned before the Middlesex County Court in 1656, confessed that "by . . . [my] sin I have not only done what I can to pull down judgment from the Lord on myself but also upon the place where I live." But Tryal Pore's tearful confession convinced the magistrates of her repentance, and they were more than ready to forgive her.

" . . . I have no pleasure in the death of the wicked, but that the wicked turn from his way and live . . ." (Ezekiel 33:11).

The Puritan magistrates, whose law book was the Bible, were generally far more anxious to see a sinner come to repentance than to mete out punishment.

In case after case, the mercy, forgiveness, and pastoral concern for the defendant stand out. Yet to any modern writer who has a streak of rebellion in him, the discipline is all he sees, and the mention of discipline these days is like waving the proverbial red flag. In fact, rebellion has been so romanticized in recent years that in our time church discipline is literally unheard of. Today, if anyone were threatened with dismissal from church membership, in all probability he would simply laugh, take up his coat, and leave.

But it was a different matter three centuries ago. First a church covenanted together, *then* the town formed around it. And under those circumstances, excommunication was a matter of the utmost gravity. It meant that the local body of Christ, after repeatedly trying to bring a sinner to repentance so he or she could receive God's forgiveness, would finally have no choice but to break fellowship with the individual and turn the person over to his or her sin. This meant that person would be under Satan's influence, and for those who know the reality of the Devil, this was a fearsome turn of events indeed! . . .

When it came to their closest relationships, the Puritans were realists in life, as well as in death. They believed that their covenant relationship with God included their children, and because they loved them, they were no more tolerant of sin in their children's lives than in their own. They would deal with sinfulness in their children as strongly as the situation required, regardless of how the children might respond at the moment.

And here is the greatest difference between the Puritans and most present-day American parents. For we are not willing to risk losing the "love" in our relationship with our children by persevering with them in matters of discipline. The biggest single cause of the breakdown of the American family is that so much of what we could call *love*, the Puritans would have another name for: *idolatry*. . . .

Authority and Order

The Puritans saw very clearly that authority, whether spiritual or temporal, invariably began in the home. "Well-ordered families naturally produce a good order in society," said Cotton Mather succinctly, and James Fitch echoed him: "Such as families are, such at last the Church and Commonwealth must be." This is obviously every bit as true today, but in Puritan New England, they took care to make sure that discipline and authority in the homes was all that it should be. For in the end a lax or loose home hurt them all, being a sin against God's plan, to say nothing of a social menace. Thus, if parents ever reached the point where they were drinking heavily, or whoring, or abusing their children, the children would be taken out of their homes and put into homes where they would receive the love (including correction) which they needed.

A great deal of emphasis was put on this matter of parental responsibility. Parents of stable families were expected to take in single men and women and raise them as part of their families, with the newcomers submitting to the heads of the house as if they were their own parents. There was even a law which required that any single person who could not afford to support a home of his own in proper order, had to live with one of the town families. In almost all cases, this proved to be a great blessing, providing a warm family environment (i.e., people who cared) which the single person did not have and often had never experienced.

The Puritan way may seem foreign to our modern American family ways, but the quality of genuine Christian love and caring for one another's souls which so characterized the family lives of our forefathers, may well contain the beginnings of answers to our own family problems. . . .

Church Life

"Gather my saints unto me. . . ." In Puritan New England, the saints gathered on the Lord's Day in the meetinghouse, the hub of their covenant life together. They came to worship the Lord and to be taught from His Word. Such was their hunger for the Word of God and for sound teaching to assist them in their struggle against sin and self, that surprising as it may seem by today's standards, (when if the pastor goes one minute beyond the stroke of noon, the congregation starts getting restless, because the turkey will get overdone, or because the first football game comes on at one), the Puritans welcomed sermons lasting two hours or more. In top form, their own pastor could be counted on, in the course of a sermon, for at least two turns of the large hourglass that stood in plain view near the pulpit—and then another turn and a half worth of prayers! And if a visiting preacher gave out after only three-quarters of an hour or so, they spoke of him as they might of a spavined horse which had given out between the stays.

The man who turned the hourglass was the Army of Christ's sergeant-at-arms, the redoubtable tithingman. He had many responsibilities in addition to turning the glass. It was he who checked the local inns on Sunday, to make sure they stayed closed, and it was he who stopped by the houses of known truants to make certain that they were in their appointed pews. But above all, it was he who was responsible for keeping the saints alert in their pews, as Pastor went from his "Thirteenthly" to his "Fourteenthly" (or, heaven forfend, from his "Twenty-seventhly" to his "Twenty-eighthly," which had been known to happen). Drugged by a lazy summer day, with the sound of crickets mingling with the "howsomesoevers," even the most zealous Puritan had been known to nod off.

But the tithingman, ever watchful for the saint who was "only resting his eyes," was equal to his task. He had a staff to discomfort them, usually with a foxtail or pheasant feather on one end for the ladies, and a brass knob on the other for the men. It should be noted that the tithingman was not imposed upon the congregation by some ecclesiastical or civil authority; rather, he was paid by the church members themselves. For such was their desire to learn from their pastor that they did not want to miss anything due to a betrayal of their flesh. Few Americans have better understood the meaning of Jesus' words to His disciples, "The spirit is willing, but the flesh is weak."

Although they were indeed serious about the importance of their spiritual life together, they were not as the present-day image would have them: taking themselves so seriously that they were incapable of laughing at themselves. In fact, the exact opposite was the case. They had a hearty appreciation of the silly incidents our foibles can cause, and laughter was a frequent visitor in their meetinghouses.

The tithingman in Lynn had a sharp thorn on the end of his staff for those whose sleep was especially sound. We are indebted to the journal of one Obadiah Turner for the following eyewitness account of what happened in church on the first Sunday in June, 1646.

> As he strutted about the meetinghouse, he did spy Mr. Tomlins sleeping with much comfort, his head kept steady by being in the corner, and his hand grasping the rail. And so spying, Allen [the tithingman] did quickly thrust his staff behind Dame Ballard and give him a grievous prick upon the hand. Whereupon Mr. Tomlins did spring up much above the floor, and with terrible force did strike his hand against the wall, and also, to the great wonder of all, did profanely exclaim, *"Curse ye, woodchuck!"* he dreaming, so it seemed, that a woodchuck had seized and bit his hand. But on coming to know where he was, and the great scandal he had committed, he seemed much abashed, but did not speak. And I think he will not soon again go to sleep in meeting.

"Calvinism ... saw too little good in human nature to trust the multitude of the unregenerate; and this lack of faith was to entail grave consequences upon the development of New England."

The Principles of Puritanism Would Be a Destructive Influence

Vernon Louis Parrington

As a Pulitzer Prize-winning historian of American intellectual life, Vernon Louis Parrington combined interpretive concepts of the liberal Jeffersonian tradition, midwestern radical Populism, and modern economic determinism. In the following viewpoint, Parrington considers the origins of New England Puritanism in the context of Puritan theologian John Calvin's belief and political practices. The Puritan theocracy, Parrington contends, provided a rationale for repressive authority in the early white settlement of America.

As you read, consider the following questions:

1. Why, according to Parrington, was "Calvinism no friend to equalitarianism"? Why does he say that Calvin was a logician, rather than a philosopher?
2. How did the Puritans deal with the hostility between Calvinist dogma and individual freedom?
3. Why, in Parrington's view, was New England Puritanism so favorable to authoritarian beliefs and practices?

Excerpts from *Main Currents in American Thought: An Interpretation of American Literature from the Beginnings to 1920, Volume III, 1860-1920, the Beginnings of Critical Realism in America* by Vernon Louis Parrington, copyright 1930 by Harcourt Brace & Company and renewed 1958 by V.L. Parrington, Jr., reprinted by permission of the publisher.

The far-reaching liberalisms implicit in the rejection of a hierarchical organization of the church were to discover no allies in the major premises of the system of theology accepted generally by the English Puritans, and by them transported to New England. Calvinism was no friend of equalitarianism. It was rooted too deeply in the Old Testament for that, was too rigidly aristocratic. It saw too little good in human nature to trust the multitude of the unregenerate; and this lack of faith was to entail grave consequences upon the development of New England. That the immigrant Puritans brought in their intellectual luggage the system of Calvin rather than of Luther must be reckoned a misfortune, out of which flowed many of the bickerings and much of the intolerance that left a stain on the pages of early New England history. . . .

Calvinism

There was scant room in the rigid system of John Calvin for Christian liberty. The Genevan thinker was a logician rather than a philosopher, a rigorous system-maker and dogmatist who knotted every argument and tied every strand securely into its fellow, till there was no escape from the net unless one broke through the mesh. To the formalist who demanded an exact system, and to the timid who feared free speculation, the logical consistency of Calvinism made irresistible appeal; and this perhaps suffices to explain its extraordinary hold on the rank and file of middle-class English Presbyterians. More original minds might break with it—men like Richard Hooker and Roger Williams and Vane and Milton—but academic thinkers and schoolmen, men whom the free spaces of thought frightened and who felt safe only behind secure fences, theologians like John Cotton and his fellows, made a virtue of necessity and fell to declaiming on the excellence of those chains wherewith they were bound. How narrow and cold was their prison they seem never to have realized; but that fact only aggravated the misfortunes that New England was to suffer from the spiritual guidance of such teachers. In seeking for an explanation of the unhappy union of a reactionary theology and a revolutionary political theory, Harriet Beecher Stowe suggested in *Poganuc People* that the Puritan immigrants were the children of two different centuries; that from the sixteenth century they got their theology, and from the seventeenth their politics, with the result that an older absolutist dogma snuggled down side by side in their minds with a later democratic conception of the state and society. In England the potential hostility between Calvinist dogma and individual freedom was perceived by the more liberal Separatists, but in America it was not till the rise of the Revolutionary disputes of the next century that Calvinism was discovered to be the foe of democratic liberalism and was finally rejected. It is a fruitful suggestion, and in its major contention that the liberalisms implicit in the Puritan revolution were ill served by a reactionary theology, it is certainly in harmony with the fact. . . .

Puritanism Denounced Freedom

Here was one of the best parts of the whole continent being monopolized by a band of people who rejected, oppressed, and banished others, or at least deprived them of all political rights, not because they were undesirable citizens, not because they were immoral, but because they refused to conform to the peculiar church polity and doctrine which the first settlers had evolved in the American wilderness. . . . The voices that pleaded for religious toleration, for civil liberty, and for a religion of love, were silenced. The intellectual life of the colony ceased to be troubled and entered into peace, but it was the peace of death.

James Truslow Adams, *The Founding of New England*, 1921.

The capable leaders who created the early institutions of Massachusetts Bay colony were Jacobean Englishmen of middle station, halfway between the aristocrat and the burgess, with certain salient characteristics of both. Fashioned by a caste society, they transported to the little commonwealth an abundant heritage of class prejudice. They aspired to be reckoned gentlemen and to live in the new world as they had lived in the old, in a half feudal state, surrounded by many servants and with numerous dependents. They honored rank, were sticklers for precedence, respected class distinctions, demanded the hereditary rights of the gentry. They had been bred up in a static order where gentlemen ruled and the people obeyed, and they could not think in terms of the Plymouth plantation covenant, subscribed by all heads of families. To the modern reader of his journal there is something almost childish in Winthrop's insistence on public deference to his official position and his grief when the halberd-bearers refused to provide the usual formality to his little progresses. But if they aspired to be rated as gentlemen, there was much also of the burgess nature in them. They were potential capitalists, eager to accumulate ample landholdings, keen to drive a bargain, given to trade and with as sharp an eye to the main chance as any London merchant. The community of goods that marked the early days of Plymouth they disliked so greatly as to account it almost sinful. In the infancy of the settlement they entered upon an active mercantile life, building their ships for the West Indian trade, joining in the fisheries off the Newfoundland coast, venturing far in pursuit of gain. Active, capable men, excellent administrators rather than speculative thinkers, stewards of the public interests as well as their own, they would take it ill to have their matured plans interfered with by busybodies and incompetents. Their own counsel sufficed them and they wanted no help from outsiders.

Endow such men with religious zeal; let them regard themselves as particular repositories of righteousness; give them a free hand to work out their program unhampered by rival policies; provide them with a handbook elaborated in complete detail by a master system-maker; and the result was certain. Their Utopia must be a close-knit church-state, with authority reserved to the aristocracy of Christian talent. It is needless to inquire whether a definite conception of a theocracy was in their minds before their coming over; some such order was clearly implicit in their religious fervor, their Hebraic theology, their Genevan discipline, their aristocratic prejudices. They might nominally accept the Plymouth model of church-government, but they would meddle with democracy in church and state no more than necessity compelled. Circumstances, as well as their own promptings, would counsel quite an opposite course. They were engaged in a difficult and perilous undertaking, begird by wilderness enemies, and fearful of hostile interference by the home authorities. If the venture were to survive, a drift towards centralization of power was as natural as it was inevitable. The common security would not suffer any dispersion of forces or domestic bickerings over authority. Dissatisfied members must be held in subjection and dangerous swarmings from the mother-hive must be prevented. The principle of Separatism was too disruptive to insure cohesive solidarity; the parts must be welded into a protective whole; and for such business what ideal was more efficient than a theocracy with Jehovah substituted for King Charles—not openly and seditiously, but quietly, in the hearts of the people. The historian need not wander far in search of the origin of the theocratic principle; it is to be found in the self-interest of the lay and clerical leaders. Ambitious men could not have devised a fitter means to weld together the two groups of magistrates and ministers, and endow their charter prerogatives with divine sanction. . . .

A Utopian Venture

Later critics of Puritanism discover in the theocratic experiment of Massachusetts Bay a preposterous attempt to turn back the pages of history, and refashion Englishmen after an ungainly Hebraic pattern. But to the leaders of that experiment it seemed rather a Utopian venture to create in the new world a nobler social order than elsewhere existed. Whether such a society was either possible or desirable, has long since become only an academic question; what is more suggestive is the fact that in spite of some bitterness on the part of a small minority, the stewardship of an oligarchy remained the accepted principle of government in Massachusetts Bay until the vacating of the charter in 1684. That it lingered out so long a life is a testimony to the skillful opportunism of the leaders. They early adopted a strategic policy which the British ministry foolishly refused to adopt a hundred years later; they cautiously undermined any potential disaffection by admitting the wealthiest and most influential to the rights of freemen, thus allying the ambitious and capable members of society with the ruling group, and laying the foundations of a provincial aristocracy, which in the course of time would secularize the government and substitute an economic for a theocratic basis of authority.

"As the clerics of [cultural] diversity indoctrinate new generations into the Orwellian official history, even the memory of what America once was will be lost."

The U.S. Must Restrict Immigration to Prevent Cultural Disintegration

Lawrence Auster

Lawrence Auster is a writer living in New York City. He attended Columbia University and the University of Colorado, where he received a B.A. in English. His articles have appeared in *National Review* and *Measure*. In the following viewpoint, he argues that immigration threatens the natural integrity of American culture, and cites such Founding Fathers as Jefferson and Hamilton as his authorities for such concerns. We are, Auster says, reaching a state of society where such cultural images as once famous Greek sculptures or Renaissance paintings of the Christ child will no longer be commonly recognizable.

As you read, consider the following questions:

1. What does Auster mean by "liberal assimilationism"? How, in his view, does it promote "inverse colonialism"?
2. What examples from art does the author cite to define our "cultural identity"?
3. Why, says Auster, "does every other country in the world have the right to preserve its identity and the United States does not"? What does he believe will be the result of this?

From Lawrence Auster, *The Path to National Suicide*, published by the American Immigration Control Foundation. Reprinted with permission.

The combined forces of open immigration and multicultural-ism constitute a mortal threat to American civilization. At a time when unprecedented ethnic diversity makes the affirma-tion of a common American culture more important than ever, we are, under the pressure of that diversity, abandoning the very idea of a common culture. "We are asking America to open its linguistic frontiers," one multiculturalist spokesman has said, "and to accept an expanded idea of what it means to be an American"—a standard that, in terms of immigration and lan-guage policies, seems to include everyone in the universe. Whether we consider America's porous borders; or the disap-pearing standards for naturalization; or the growth of official multilingualism; or the new "diversity" curricula aimed at de-stroying the basis of common citizenship; or the extension of virtually all the rights and protections of citizenship to legal *and* illegal aliens; or the automatic granting of citizenship to children of illegals; the tendency is clear: we have in effect redefined the nation to the point where there is no remaining criterion of American identity other than the physical fact of one's being here. It is, to quote Alexander Hamilton, "an attempt to break down every pale which has been erected for the preservation of a national spirit and a national character."

Expectations About Immigrants

The irony is that most Americans support immigration as a "lib-eral" policy. That is, they want America to remain open and to help people, and they also expect that the new immigrants will assimilate into our existing society. It was on this basis that the opening of America's doors to every country on earth was ap-proved in 1965 and continues to enjoy unassailable political sup-port. But we are beginning to see, simply as a practical, human matter, that the successful assimilation of such huge numbers of widely diverse peoples into a single people and a viable polity is a pipe dream. It is at this point that multiculturalism comes along and says: "That's not a problem. We don't want to assimilate into this oppressive, Eurocentered mold. We want to reconstruct America as a multicultural society." And this radical pluralist view gains acceptance by retaining the moral legitimacy, the patina of humanitarianism, that properly belonged to the older liberalism which it has supplanted. We have thus observed the progress, largely unperceived by the American people, from the liberal assimilationist view, which endorses open immigration be-cause it naively believes that our civilization can survive unlim-ited diversity, to radical multiculturalism, which endorses open immigration because it wants our civilization to end.

What has been said so far will doubtless offend those who see unlimited diversity not as a threat to our society, but as a glorious enhancement of it. I do not deny that there are many apparently positive things associated with our expanding demographic character: the stimulus of the boundless human variety in our big cities; the satisfaction of welcoming people from every country in the world and seeing them do well here; the heady sense that we are moving into a New Age in which all barriers between people will disappear and humanity will truly be one. But the question must be asked: is all this excitement about a New Age, this fascination with the incredible changes occurring before our eyes, a sound basis for determining our national destiny? Is all this idealism without its dark side? Is it not to be feared—if the lessons of history are any guide—that the "terrible and magnificent struggle" to recreate America is leading us, not to the post-imperialist age of peace and love the cultural pluralists dream of, but to a new and more terrible age of ethnic imperialism?

The Ethnic Problem

Many Americans (including myself) find offensive the notion that the government should consider the spelling of a last name or the facial features of an applicant in awarding entry visas. But to ignore the "ethnic problem" at a time when long-dormant ethnic conflicts are being rekindled around the world is simply to bury one's head in the sand. Ethnicity matters, and it matters for a very long time.

George J. Borjas, *National Review*, February 1, 1993.

Americans are being told that to redeem themselves from their past sins, they must give way to, and even merge with, the cultures they have oppressed or excluded in the past. But for a culture to deny its own "false" legitimacy, as America is now called upon to do, does not create a society free of false legitimacy; it simply means creating a vacuum of legitimacy—and thus a vacuum of power—into which other cultures, replete with their own "imperialistic lies," will move. Training Hispanic and other immigrant children in American public schools to have their primary loyalty to their native cultures is not to create a new kind of bicultural, cosmopolitan citizenry; it is to systematically downgrade our national culture while raising the status and power of other cultures. As James Burnham has shown in *The Machiavellians*, we need to see the *real* meaning (a concern with power) that is concealed behind the *formal* meaning of various idealistic slogans. The *formal* meaning of "diversity," "cultural equity," "gorgeous mosaic" and so on is a society in which many different cultures will live together in perfect equality and peace (i.e., a society that has never existed and never will exist); the *real* meaning of these slogans is that the power of the existing mainstream society to determine its own destiny shall be drastically reduced while the power of other groups, formerly marginal or external to that society, will be increased. In other words, the U.S. must, in the name of diversity, abandon *its* particularity while the very groups making that demand shall hold on to *theirs*.

Thus understood, cultural pluralism is not the innocent expansion of our human sympathies it pretends to be, but a kind of inverse colonialism. *Time*, in a special issue put together by its Hispanic staff writers, speaks buoyantly of the coming "convergence" of American and Hispanic cultures, a convergence that Americans should welcome "unconditionally" as an enrichment of their own society and as an opening up of their "restricted" identity. "We come bearing gifts," *Time* says on behalf of the growing Hispanic presence in the United States. But, stripped of its sentimentality, isn't this what colonial powers have always said? The only difference is that, in the Age of Imperialism, it was the strong powers that took over the weak; in today's Age of Diversity, it is the weak who are taking over the strong, with the strong's invitation and blessing.

An additional irony is that the call for cultural pluralism is often accompanied by a call for *globalism*—which would obviously tend to weaken *national* diversity. If diversity means anything (as distinguished from its Burnhamite "real" meaning), it means that each nation maintains its own identity. If different societies blend together, or if one of them, through mass migration or cultural imperialism, imposes its identity on another, the result is a loss of national identity and therefore a loss of diversity. As John Ney has observed: "In any objective study of cultural dynamics, is not cultural co-existence a myth? Does not one culture or the other triumph, or merge in a synthesis in which neither (or none) survives intact?" If it is diversity we really want, we should preserve our own and each other's distinct national identities. But if the relationship we desire between foreign cultures and our own is "convergence" (*Time*'s upbeat motto for the Latin American invasion), then we should recognize that this means the end of American civilization as we know it.

The Loss of Cultural Identity

To picture the spiritual impact that the multicultural revolution will have on our society would require an act of historical imagination that is frankly beyond the power of this writer. Indeed, it is this inability to "imagine" our own cultural heritage and what its loss would mean to us—largely a result of several

59

generations of relativist education and the triumph of pop culture—that makes it hard for us to articulate or defend that heritage. As John Lukacs has written: "It is a problem of existing cultural essences and assets that cannot be quantified or computerized. . . . What is threatened is not just our nation's body, but its soul. Perhaps I can illustrate what I mean through the example of art. When we look at an ancient Greek sculpture, or a Renaissance painting showing a group of people gathered around the Christ child, or, for that matter, a Hollywood classic from the thirties, we are seeing profoundly resonant images of our own civilization and culture, images that have made us what we are. Looking at the Renaissance painting or the Greek sculpture, we realize that we are partakers of the same Classical, Judeo-Christian, Western heritage, actors in the same drama. This vital communication of one generation, one age with another is the soul of civilization. From it we derive the sense of being part of a continuum which stretches back to the ancient past and forward to the future. From that vital intercourse with the past each generation renews itself."

Immigration and Welfare

The American experience with immigration has been a triumphant success. . . . But in the late twentieth century, the economic and political culture of the U.S. has changed significantly—from classical liberalism to an interventionist welfare statism. In the previous two hundred years of U.S. history, a number of tried-and-true, but undeniably tough, techniques of assimilation had been perfected. Today, they have been substantially abandoned. Earlier waves of immigrants were basically free to succeed or fail. And many failed: as much as a third of the 1880-to-1920 immigrants returned to their native lands. But with the current wave, public policy interposes itself, with the usual debatable results.

Peter Brimelow, *National Review*, June 22, 1992.

But now this continuum, which is the body of our civilization extending through time, is about to be broken forever. Under the pressure of multiculturalism, Americans will be denied their own heritage and prevented from handing it on to succeeding generations. Because that entire cultural heritage, which (before the opening up of massive Third-World immigration) was taken for granted as "our" heritage, is now considered to be merely an exclusive, "white" heritage and therefore *illegitimate*. Deprived of its *good conscience*, American/Western culture will lose the ability to defend itself and will be progressively downgraded to accommodate a bewildering array of other cultures. "In its Third Century," Kotkin and Kishimoto write, "American culture may no longer be based predominantly on European themes. Its motifs may be as much Latin or Asian as traditional Anglo-American." As the image of our civilization, as expressed in the arts and literature, changes to a multiracial, multicultural image, what kind of art will result? Movies and plays, instead of portraying the relationships of individuals within a community or family, as drama has done time out of mind, must focus self-consciously on race relations. Established literary works that have formed a living bridge between one generation of Americans and the next will fall into oblivion, to be replaced by works on minority, Hispanic and Asian issues. The religious paintings of the multiculturalist society, instead of portraying a group of individuals chosen from the artists' imagination, would follow a statistical formula; the figures gathered around the Christ child would have to be x percent brown, x percent black, yellow, white and so on, all chosen on the basis of racial balance rather than their individual character. Diversity would so overwhelm unity that the idea of diversity within unity would be lost. If you think this is an absurd prediction about the future of art and of society, just look at any television show or advertisement. The formulaic racial balance imposes itself everywhere, even to the point of inventing multiracial families on television that don't exist in the real world. It is the new image of America, popularized by *Time* covers and ABC News graphics—a brown, mixed people, painted in a heroic, proletarian style that might be called Multiracialist Realism. . . .

The End of American Civilization

I have been attempting to suggest a few of the myriad potential effects of mass immigration and multiculturalism on this country's future. There are darker scenarios I have not explored—the spread of Third-World conditions in parts of our country; the collapse of civic order (nightmarishly portrayed in Tom Wolfe's *Bonfire of the Vanities*), or the disintegration of the United States along regional and ethnic lines. Whatever the future America may look like, it will not be a country that we—or our forebears whose legacy we are so carelessly throwing away—would be able to recognize.

In the years and decades to come, as the present American people and their descendants begin to understand what is happening to their country; as they see their civilization disappearing piece by piece, city by city, state by state, from before their eyes, and that nothing can be done to stop it, they will suffer the same collapse of spirit that occurs to any people when its way of life, its historical identity, is taken away from it. Beneath all the hopeful names they will try to find for these changes—diversity, world-nation, global oneness—there will be the repressed knowledge that America is becoming an utterly different country from what it has been, and that this means the end of their world. But the pain will not last for long. As the clerics of diversity indoctrinate new generations into the Orwellian official history, even the memory of what America once was will be lost.

Finally, if we want to consider "cultural equity," there seems to be an extraordinary kind of *inequity* in the proposition that the United States must lose its identity, must become the "speechless, meaningless country" that Allan Bloom has foreseen, while the countries that the new immigrants are coming from are free to preserve *their* identities. In a hundred years, the United States will have become in large part an Hispanic nation, while Latin America will still be what it has always been; Mexico has strict immigration laws even against other Latin Americans. China, Korea, the Philippines and India will still have their historic cultures intact after having exported millions of their people to America, while America's historic culture will have vanished. If the situation were reversed and North Americans were colonizing Latin America and Asia, it would be denounced as racist imperialism. Why, then, does every other country in the world have the right to preserve its identity but the United States has not? The answer, as I've tried to show, is that the end of multiculturalism is not some utopian, "equal" society, but simply the end of American civilization.

So much for America; if other Western nations continue *their* openness to Third-World immigration, we may be witnessing the beginning of the end of Western civilization as a whole. And this defeat of the West will have been accomplished, not by the superior strength or civilization of the newcomers, not by the "forces of history," but simply by the feckless generosity and moral cowardice of the West itself. In the prophetic words of social psychologist William McDougall:

> As I watch the American nation speeding gaily, with invincible optimism down the road to destruction, I seem to be contemplating the greatest tragedy in the history of mankind.

"The fundamental multiculturalism of Western culture . . . has been constructed out of a fusion of disparate and often conflicting cultural traditions."

The U.S. Must Embrace Diverse Cultural Influences

Reed Way Dasenbrock

In creating the intellectual and political culture of the American revolution, figures like Paine and Jefferson came to consider themselves "citizens of the world." In the following viewpoint, Reed Way Dasenbrock, a professor of English at New Mexico State University, reviews the long creation of "Western culture," and argues that it has always evolved from different cultures, freely drawing on a number of traditions. The Greeks, for instance, clearly depended on Egypt for a number of mathematical and intellectual achievements. While cautioning against a superficial treatment of complex historical realities, Dasenbrock believes that the main direction of our cultural development today is positive and worldwide in scope.

As you read, consider the following questions:

1. Why, says Dasenbrock, is "Western culture itself an example of multiculturalism"? What were some of the contributions of other societies to our culture?
2. What is the difference between a normative and a descriptive concept of culture?
3. Where does Dasenbrock believe we should turn for evidence of what a new, emerging multiculturalism will look like?

From Reed Way Dasenbrock, "The Multicultural West," *Dissent*, Fall 1991. Reprinted with permission.

When we speak of a common Western culture or, more narrowly, of a common European culture, we are speaking of something that took millennia to construct and consolidate. There was no common European identity two thousand years ago, just a collection of disparate peoples and cultures ranging from the world's most powerful and sophisticated, the Roman Empire, to the rude Germanic and Celtic peoples of the North. By now, it is those rude, uncivilized people who seem to stand at the center of European culture. Joseph Conrad's brilliant frame for *Heart of Darkness* reminds his British readers of 1900 that Britain, by then the very center of European civilization, was once also a "heart of darkness," considered by its Roman conquerors to lie at the outer edges of civilization.

Cultural Imitation

What created the relative coherence of European culture we see today out of this multiplicity of peoples, cultures, and traditions? Contemporary thinking usually answers, *domination*—assuming that we always go on being ourselves until someone else overpowers us. However, though force undoubtedly played a role, Europe did not take shape primarily through conquest or forcible assimilation. (The Roman conquest of Britain left a few ruins but had little lasting effect.) It was created primarily by cultural imitation, the mysterious process by which one culture responds to the influence of another. Indeed, the key moment in the creation of a European culture was not the initial sudden emergence of essential Western concepts such as democracy in Athenian Greece. It was, instead, the more gradual process by which another society—Rome—underwent Hellenization and took over Greek ideals and culture as its own. Differences remained, but cultural influence and imitation created a degree of commonality such that we can speak with some accuracy of a shared Greco-Roman or classical civilization. Virgil thus is in a sense more important in the creation of "Western" culture than Homer precisely because of his acceptance of Homer as a normative ideal. This process of imitation, repeated many times over, gives birth to the essential Western concept that culture is not autochthonous, that it comes from somewhere else: from the East, if one is a Midwesterner or Westerner; from Europe, if one is American or Russian or Australian; from the Continent, if one is British; from the Mediterranean, if one is Nordic; from Greece, if one was Roman. Culture thus is not what we do but usually what someone else does better than we do. This relation is always double-edged: the provincial side both resents and admires the sophisticated side in the relationship. But there is never any ambiguity about which is the sophisticated side: it is, simply, the side that is the object of imitation over the long term.

Now this sense of culture as something learned, something constructed, something that we share with and take from others, is in quite sharp contrast to the anthropological sense of culture as the ensemble of practices of a given community. The difference is between a normative, or prescriptive, and a descriptive concept. Culture in the normative sense is what we ought to do; for an anthropologist culture is what a given people do. The anthropological sense seems to govern the current use of the term among multiculturalists, particularly in their assumption that it is important to "preserve" the culture of minority students. African Americans should study African and African American literature to maintain their own cultural identity as African Americans, and it is partly for this reason that it is deemed important to have African Americans—not members of other groups—teaching these subjects. Yet the educational practice urged on the society as a whole by multiculturalists is deeply Virgilian. Multiculturalists urge members of the mainstream culture to learn about other cultures so that we can learn from them as well as learn about them. Diversity in the curriculum is seen as important because other cultures have traits to learn from; the project is for our students and our society to become more multicultural, not simply to be more informed about other cultures. And if we are to become more multicultural, then we must consciously become a combination of what we wish to retain from our culture and what we wish to adopt from that of others. We must become like Virgil. And it is for the same reason that this project is also resisted so strongly: those opposed to multiculturalism are just as Virgilian, insisting that we should model ourselves on the models we have long imitated, not on "alien" traditions and ways of being.

However, those on both sides who present Western culture and multiculturalism as if they were opposed options miss what I would call the fundamental multiculturalism of Western culture, the fact that it has been constructed out of a fusion of disparate and often conflicting cultural traditions. The straw man of the multicultural polemics is now the dead white European male or the Anglo; only twenty years ago the straw man of comparable polemics was the white Anglo-Saxon Protestant. Whatever happened to the WASP?

Differences Are Melding

In just one generation, it would seem, the once crucial distinctions between Protestant and Catholic, between Protestant and Jew, between Anglo-Saxons and other European ethnic groups have ceased to matter: all of these groups are seen to be part of a homogeneous "Eurocentric" tradition. But these internal barriers inside the "Western tradition" in America did not go away magically or easily, any more than the internal barriers inside of Europe did. One might remind anyone glibly referring to "the European tradition" (as if it were a harmonious whole) of the long conflict from 1914 to 1945 (or really from about 1500 to 1945) concerning who was to dominate Europe; one might remind anyone glibly talking about a homogeneous Anglo culture in the United States of the intense resistance, as recently as 1960, to the election of the Irish Catholic John F. Kennedy to the presidency. If we can talk about European unity or about a certain unified "Anglo" culture in this country, it is only as a result of a long historical process of knocking down the walls that have separated the different European communities. And that process is not complete even today.

Encourage Immigration

Many of us care more about making the United States a "shining city on the hill" than about the origins of the people who help attain that goal. For those who care about the strengthening of American values of liberty, constitutionalism, and democracy so that they will spread throughout the world, the most effective step is to bring persons from the rest of the world here, so that their light can go back to where they came from, and make those places more like "us."

Julian L. Simon, *National Review*, February 1, 1993.

The wall that multiculturalist slogans create between *just one* Western culture and non-Western culture thus reflects a kind of amnesia. Moreover, the disparate elements out of which "Western culture" has been created are themselves often non-Western in origin. One of the loci of the recent debates has been the argument advanced in Martin Bernal's *Black Athena* and elsewhere that classical Greek culture is deeply indebted to Egyptian (and therefore to "black") culture. The debate here is really about the extent to which Egyptian culture can be said to be African. For there is no disputing the obvious debt of Hellenic culture to ancient Egyptian and Near Eastern cultures. However the details of this particular controversy sort out, the imitativeness of Western culture—its ability to learn from cultures outside the West as well as from other places inside the West—has obviously been one of its constitutive features. We might broaden T. S. Eliot's dictum and say that "immature cultures borrow, mature cultures steal.". . .

The choice cannot be between a closed Western tradition and openness to other non-Western traditions, for the Western tradition itself has always been open—if not always prone to admit that it is—to other cultural traditions. If you changed into or out of pajamas, took a bath, brushed your teeth, or had a cup of tea or coffee this morning, each of these activities is something we have taken from Asia. If, say, William Bennett's attitudes toward other cultures had always been dominant in the West, we would still be worshipping Zeus and trying to use Roman numerals. The very spirit of the West when it encounters another cultural practice is to say, "Is there something we can use here?" Is tobacco good to smoke? Is coffee good to drink? Is chocolate good to eat? Not every borrowing has been wise, but by and large Western culture has been immeasurably enriched by its ability to adapt to and borrow from others.

If this history teaches us anything, it is that crises of multiculturalism have deep historical roots and cannot be wished away. Early medieval England was a country riven by a schism between the indigenous culture and language of the Anglo-Saxons and the imported culture and French language of the conquering Normans: what resulted was the hybrid language of English and a profoundly hybrid and syncretic culture. Multiculturalism has emerged in the United States today out of a comparable historical exigency. On the one hand, we are faced with a new wave of immigration into the United States: our country is becoming less European, less white, more Asian and more Latin American. Europe, having for decades felt smug and superior about racial problems and tensions in America, is faced with the same phenomenon and is—if anything—considerably less prepared to deal with it. On the other hand, we and every other trading nation are faced with an increasingly integrated world, above all an increasingly integrated international economy, in which we can no longer pretend to separate ourselves from other nations. Borders are now gates, not walls, through which pour problems—drugs and too many Toyotas—but also essential ingredients such as oil. Most important, across borders now pour people. And each of these tendencies is likely to become more pronounced, not less, for the foreseeable future. How do we respond to the complex interaction of cultures that shapes the contemporary world? My answer may seem paradoxical: we need to adopt a good deal of the multiculturalist agenda precisely because it is in keeping with the best and most important aspects of Western and American culture. The great moments of our historical tradition have been moments of contact with and borrowing from other cultures: a good deal of what was important about the Middle Ages was prompted by contact with Islamic civilization: Greek exiles in Italy helped spark the Renaissance, as did the discovery of the New World; the discovery of the spiritual traditions of Asia played an important role in

British and particularly American romanticism. Our historical situation is perhaps more complex than any of these, since we are now in contact with the entire world through immigration and trade, but it is nevertheless a situation these examples will help us to understand. When faced with disparate cultures in contact (which usually means conflict), the successful response has always been assimilative and syncretic, to mix and match, taking the best of each. We now need to do this with the totality of the cultures of the world. But this doesn't represent a surrender of the Western tradition as much as a reaffirmation of it. . . .

The Benefits of the Melting Pot

I think we are the first universal nation, that the melting pot is working, and that we are creating—through immigration and intermarriage—a new folk that will be a model for mankind.

Ben J. Wattenberg, *National Review*, February 1, 1993.

We are in for a period of experimentation, and we can only hope that more complex models and pedagogies slowly emerge and replace the simplistic visions and responses of both sides in the current debate. To anyone searching in the interim for what such a multiculturalism would look like, my advice is to read contemporary non-Western literature written in English, which seems to me to be a crucial site where we can move toward a more sophisticated sense of the world's cultures. English is an international language, playing an important role inside about one fourth of the world's 160 countries, and it has therefore become an important international literary language. Important—great—writing is being done in English all over the world, on every continent today. But this body of literature has not yet played an important role in the curriculum at any level, since it doesn't seem English or American enough to make it into the English curriculum, or "different enough" to make it into those parts of the curriculum concerned with other cultures. In this context, that is precisely its virtue. The writers themselves are often attacked from both sides, precisely because they don't fit into one camp or the other, as the case of Salman Rushdie has shown most spectacularly. In fact, the discussion about "Afrocentricity" took shape first in literary criticism when critics such as Chinweizu attacked Wole Soyinka and other African writers for their "Euromodernism." Yet the bridges these writers are building, by importing European forms into non-European contexts and by introducing non-European cultural traditions into European languages, may in retrospect seem as crucial to the formation of a world culture as the Augustan imitation of Greek culture was for the formation of classical culture and the Renaissance imitation of those classical forms and of Italian culture was for the construction of European culture.

I believe the construction of a world culture—as Wyndham Lewis said more than forty years ago and V. S. Naipaul has recently reiterated—is the task that now faces us. Despite the fashionable nostalgia for pockets of difference yet unintegrated into a world community, the alternative to such a world culture is not a lively diversity of cultures as much as unending conflict among them. Will pointing this out magically transform the current debate into a less shrill one? Of course not, for there are powerful reasons why each side in this debate wants not to understand the other. On the one hand, advocates of a separatist cultural identity for minorities reserve their harshest criticism for those of their own communities like Naipaul or Richard Rodriguez who insist that a measure of assimilation is inevitable, that accommodation must be a two-way street. Ayatollah Khomeini's condemnation of Salman Rushdie is the most conspicuous exemplification of this rage: that one of "us" could be "polluted" by contact with the other side. On the other hand, a George Will or a William Bennett finds it hard to admit that the West might have something to learn from as well as something to teach the rest of the world.

My point is not just that both sides hold to blindingly narrow ideals. It is rather that neither side perceives the world in which we live. Despite all of the talk on both sides about preserving earlier cultural identities, these identities are changing quickly and inexorably. It is in this sense that—despite the apparent polarization of the debate—the two sides are really one. Together, they represent a point of view that is historically irrelevant.

Periodical Bibliography

The following articles have been selected to supplement the diverse views presented in this chapter.

James Atlas — "Chicago's Grumpy Guru [Allan Bloom]," *The New York Times Magazine*, January 3, 1988.

Benjamin Barber — "The Philosopher Despot," *Harper's*, January 1988.

Allan Bloom — "A Most Uncommon Scold," *Time*, October 17, 1988.

Martin Gardner — "Giving God a Hand," *New York Review of Books*, August 13, 1987.

William Greider — "Bloom and Doom," *Rolling Stone*, October 8, 1987.

Kenneth Hovey — "The Great Books Versus America," *Profession*, 1988.

Everett Ladd — "Secular and Religious America," *Society*, March/April 1987.

Delos B. McKown — "Religion and the Constitution," *The Humanist*, May/June 1988.

Martin Marty — "Public Religion: The Republican Banquet," *Phi Beta Kappa Journal*, Winter 1988.

Newsweek — "Talking to God," January 6, 1992.

Robert Scholes — "Three Views of Education: Nostalgia, History, and Voodoo," *College English* (50), 1988.

Peter Steinfels — "Beliefs: Two Authors' Contention Has Set Off a Debate," *The New York Times*, February 20, 1993.

Robert Sullivan — "An Army of the Faithful," *The New York Times Magazine*, April 25, 1993.

Time — "One Nation, Under God," December 9, 1991.

Voice Literary Supplement — "Oh, God! Varieties of Religious Experience," February 1993.

William Williamson — "Is the U.S.A. a Christian Nation?" *Free Inquiry*, Spring 1993.

Kenneth Woodward — "Losing Our Moral Umbrella," *Newsweek*, December 7, 1992.

Are Diverse Traditions Fairly Represented in American Education?

CULTURE
WARS

VERNON REGIONAL
JUNIOR COLLEGE LIBRARY

Chapter Preface

What is taught and what should be tolerated are feverish issues in American education today. Campuses have become increasingly politicized over issues involving curriculum, admission of minority students (and respect for minority cultures), women's rights, and other cultural debates. Institutions such as schools and colleges began to change dramatically in the 1960s, when faced with the urgent demands of Chicano and black power movements for recognition of the validity of their history and culture. The aims of these groups are echoed today among advocates of multiculturalism: to break down stereotypes and misconceptions.

The intensity of these disputes resembles theological controversies of former times; even the language is similar. For instance, one of the key words in contemporary educational controversies is the "canon," which originally referred to those books finally agreed upon for inclusion in the Bible. In our own times, we argue which books are essential—"canonical"—for the curricula of our schools and colleges. In A.D. 1215, authorities at the University of Paris tried to prevent the study of Aristotle because they feared that his concepts of logic would lead to a questioning of Christian beliefs. The Thirty Years' War devastated much of Europe in the seventeenth century, because of disputes on religious questions such as whether Protestant or Catholic authority should prevail in a given nation. Now we debate such matters as the contributions that African-Americans have made to our culture, or whether certain expressions might be offensive to women. In the place of theological correctness, we must now deal with the concept of political correctness. The similarity of the language perhaps reflects the deep devotion each side feels toward its cause, making compromise even more difficult.

The authors of this chapter consider a wide range of issues that bear on the present status and future of American education.

VERNON REGIONAL
JUNIOR COLLEGE LIBRARY

"All of these dead white males made important contributions to the pursuit of truth."

The Classic Works of Western Civilization Should Continue to Dominate Education

Mortimer Adler

Over some four decades, the Great Books of the Western World, edited by Mortimer Adler, has been a successful, if expensive, set of classic texts with considerable influence in America. When Adler developed the Great Books, he hoped that groups of citizens across the country would gather to read and discuss this set of volumes. In the following viewpoint, Adler defends the purpose and rationale of his selections for the canon.

As you read, consider the following questions:

1. How does Adler distinguish between "good" and "great" books?
2. What is Adler's view of non-Western culture?
3. What does the author mean by "restricted pluralism"?

From Mortimer J. Adler, "The Transcultural and the Multicultural." In *The Great Ideas Today 1991*, Mortimer J. Adler, ed. Reprinted with permission from *The Great Ideas Today 1991*, © 1991 by Encyclopaedia Britannica, Inc.

The controversy about multiculturalism at the college level focuses on the books that should be a part of one's general education. It is a dispute about the traditionally recognized canon of the monuments of Western literature in all fields—works of mathematics and science as well as works of poetry, drama, and fiction, and also works of biography, history, philosophy, and theology. Here we are confronted with current attacks upon the canonical list of great books and the responses that those attacks have elicited.

I am involved in this controversy—as associate editor of the first edition of the *Great Books of the Western World*, published in 1952, and as editor in chief of the second, much expanded edition, published in 1990.

The second edition differed from the first in many respects: new translations, a revised *Synopticon*, and six volumes of twentieth-century authors that did not appear in the first edition, as well as fifteen authors added in the period from Homer to Freud. As in the case of the first edition, so in the case of the second: our editorial board and the large group of advisers we consulted did not agree unanimously about the authors to be included; but in both cases there was 90-percent agreement. That, in my judgement, is all one can expect in a matter of this kind.

I would like to call attention to two things about the second edition. In writing an introductory essay, which appeared in a volume that accompanied the set titled *The Great Conversation*, I anticipated the controversy that the second edition of the *Great Books of the Western World* would arouse. This did not arise before. In the 1940s, when we were engaged in producing the first edition, *Eurocentric* was not current as a disapprobative term. There was no hue and cry about the absence of female authors; nor had blacks cried out for representation in the canon. In those earlier decades of this century, students and teachers in our colleges and educators in general were not concerned with multiculturalism in our educational offerings.

The second edition contains female authors, some in the nineteenth and some in the twentieth century, but no black authors; and it is still exclusively Western (i.e., European or American authors) with none from the four or five cultural traditions of the Far East.

The Difference Between Good and Great

The controversy over the desirability of multiculturalism having arisen in the late 1980s, I took account of it in my introductory essay, pointing out carefully the criteria in terms of which the authors were selected for inclusion, explaining the difference between the 500 or so *great* works included in the set and the thousands of *good* books listed in the recommended readings at the end of each of the 102 chapters in the *Synopticon*. These lists included many female and many black authors, but none from the Far East.

These exclusions were not, and are not, invidious. The difference between *great* and *good* books is one of kind, not of degree. Good books are not "almost great" or "less than great" books. Great books are relevant to human problems in every century, not just germane to current twentieth-century problems. A great book requires reading over and over, and has many meanings; a good book need be read no more than once, and need have no more than one meaning.

Scrapping the Classics

At some colleges and universities, traditional survey courses of world and English literature, as also of social thought, have been scrapped or diluted. At others they are in peril. At still others they will be. What replaces them is sometimes a mere option of electives, sometimes "multicultural" courses introducing material from Third World cultures and thinning out an already thin sampling of Western writings, and sometimes courses geared especially to issues of class, race, and gender.

Irving Howe, *The New Republic*, February 18, 1991.

I also explained but did not apologize for the so-called Eurocentrism of the *Great Books of the Western World* by pointing out why no authors or works from the four or five distinct cultural traditions in the Far East were included or should be included. The Western authors are engaged in a great conversation across the centuries about great ideas and issues. In the multicultural traditions of the Far East, there are, perhaps, as many as four or five great conversations about different sets of ideas, but the authors and books in these different cultural traditions do not combine these ideas in one Far Eastern tradition, nor do they participate in the great conversation that has occurred over the last twenty-five centuries in the West. There are undoubtedly great, as distinguished from good, books in all of these Far Eastern traditions.

I did not anticipate the nature of the response to the publication of the second edition by those who challenged its Eurocentrism or who complained about the fact that its authors were still for the most part dead white males, with few females and no blacks. They based their challenges on press announcements of the list of included authors, but without reading my introductory essay and without knowing that a large number of female and black authors were included in the 102 lists in the *Synopticon* of *good* books cited as readings recommended in addition to the great books included in the set, along with many other books by white males, none of them regarded as great.

I should mention one other point that is highly germane to the controversy. Many of those who criticize the traditional canon of great books and call for its rejection incorrectly suppose that its defenders claim that it is a repository of transcultural truth and nothing else. That is not the case. The editors and advisory consultants of the *Great Books of the Western World* know that there is much more error or falsity in the intellectual and cultural tradition of the West than there is truth.

The relation of truth to error is a one-to-many ratio; for every truth, there are many deviations from it that are false. What truth is to be found is, of course, transcultural. The multiple errors, some of them multicultural, that impinge on each truth are of great importance for the understanding of the truth. Without grappling with the errors, one's understanding of the truth that corrects them is shallow. It follows that if the truths to be found in the great books of the West are transcultural, so, too, must be the understanding of the errors, some of which will be discovered in the Far East.

Which Works Should Be Studied?

I turn now from the controversy about the second edition of the *Great Books of the Western World* to the controversy that has very recently arisen concerning what books should be required reading in colleges that still have some interest in the general, as opposed to the specialized, education of their students. This controversy started at Stanford University in 1988 and has spread since then to other colleges across the country.

The popular press and the electronic media have given the controversy ample notice, and its pros and cons have been publicly debated. A desirable multiculturalism has been appealed to as the basis not only for including many recent books by female, black, and non-Western authors but also for eliminating from the required readings a large number of authors and books that have long been treasured as Western greats, especially authors and books in classical antiquity, in the Middle Ages, and in modern times up to the nineteenth century.

Unquestionably among the books that have been recommended for addition, some contain recently discovered or restated truths that correct errors to be found in books of earlier centuries. If so, who could reasonably object to such additions? No one. But the same cannot be said for the recommended deletions from the list of required readings—Plato and Aristotle, for example; Herodotus, Thucydides, and Gibbon; Homer, Virgil,

Dante, Shakespeare, and Tolstoy; Marcus Aurelius, Rabelais, Montaigne, Hobbes, Locke, Rousseau, and John Stuart Mill. All of these dead white males made important contributions to the pursuit of truth, even if there was much error in their insights, their principles, or their conclusions. Why, then, should many of them, or any of them, be rejected, if their inclusion does not call for the rejection of twentieth-century books written by female or black authors?

If general education is to include not just Western civilization but the other great cultures of the world in the Far East, a question still remains. If Western civilization is included as one of many in the multicultural melange, why exclude Western authors and books long recognized as truly great for their contribution to the pursuit and understanding of truth?

It may be said, of course, that there is not enough time to include these older authors if twentieth-century authors and Far Eastern authors are also to be added to the required readings. It may be said that general education should be given up and no readings at all should be required for that purpose.

But it should not be said, as some of the proponents of multiculturalism seem to think, that truth is merely what some people assert. And that they would like to be the ones to assert what is true, or to elect those who are to assert it. Or if objective truth is held to exist somewhere, it is in natural science, but not in speculative philosophy, theology, or religion, and especially not in moral philosophy, which is concerned with questions of value—good and evil, right and wrong, what ought to be sought and done.

Multicultural Goals

For such multiculturalists, these are all held to be matters of subjective personal predilection. They are not matters of public knowledge, not even knowledge with residual doubt, but only private or individual opinion, unsupported by the weight of evidence or reasons. What is or is not desirable is, therefore, entirely a matter of taste (about which there should be no disputing), not a matter of truth that can be disputed in terms of empirical evidence and reasons.

That being the case, we are left with a question that should be embarrassing to the multiculturalists, though they are not likely to feel its pinch. When they proclaim the desirability of the multicultural, they dispute about matters that should not be disputed. What, then, can possibly be their grounds of preference? Since in their terms it cannot appeal to any relevant body of truth, what they demand in the name of multiculturalism must arise from a wish for power or self-esteem.

When dispute on a basis of empirical evidence or by appeal to rational grounds is ruled out, conflicting claims can only be resolved by power politics, either by force or by dominance of a majority. In either case, it comes down to might makes right. That is exactly what is happening today in the efforts of the multiculturalists to change the curriculum in the public schools and in our colleges.

Multiculturalism is cultural pluralism. In the twentieth century, pluralism has become part of the democratic ideal, opposed to the monolithic totalitarianism that is now being challenged in the Soviet Union, and also to the equally monolithic rigidity of Islamic, Jewish, or Christian fundamentalism.

While democracy and socialism, and with them pluralism, are ideal in the social and economic dimensions of society, cultural pluralism is not wholly desirable in other dimensions of our life. What is desirable is a *restricted* cultural pluralism; that is, the promotion and preservation of pluralism in all matters of taste, but not in any matters that are concerned with objectively valid truth, either descriptive factual truth or prescriptive normative truth.

In this century, mathematics, the hard-core natural sciences, and their attendant technologies have become transcultural. What truth they have so far attained is at present acknowledged everywhere on earth. Whether or not in the next century or in a more distant future transcultural truth will be attained in philosophy, in the social sciences, in institutional history, and even in religion is an open question that should not be dogmatically answered by the present breed of multiculturalists whose unrestricted pluralism substitutes power or might for truth and right in the effort to control what should be taught or thought.

"The world is interdependent and America is not simply a sum of marginalities."

The Classics Must Be Broadened to Include Multicultural Literature

Todd Gitlin

As a professor of sociology at the University of California at Berkeley, Todd Gitlin has written a book about the 1960s culture of rebellion called *The Sixties: Years of Hope, Days of Rage*. In the following viewpoint, he argues that modern curriculum must include more books from other cultures, while retaining the best of the European heritage.

As you read, consider the following questions:

1. What two events, according to Gitlin, have precipitated America's current identity crisis?
2. What does Gitlin mean by a "loose" canon?
3. On what points does the author agree with academic conservatives?

From Todd Gitlin, "On the Virtues of a Loose Canon," *New Perspectives Quarterly*, Summer 1991. Reprinted with permission.

I understand the "political correctness" controversy as the surface of a deeper fault line—a trauma in American cultural identity.

America's current identity crisis was precipitated by several events. First, the collapse of the Cold War denied the US an opponent in the tug-of-war between capitalism and communism. When the enemy let go of the rope, the American "team"—constituted to hold the line against tyranny—was dropped on its collective ass. We are now on the prowl for a new enemy, something or someone to mobilize against: Noriega, drugs, Satan, Saddam Hussein or the newest bogey: "political correctness"—a breed of left-wing academic intolerance and exclusion that ends up shackling not only free speech but free-flowing intellectual inquiry—a perversion of a sensible multicultural program of tolerance and inclusion.

Though political correctness is rightly condemned for its flights of excess, opponents often fail to separate multiculturalism from the PC version of tribalism. Indeed, some of the right's intolerance is aimed not at the message but at the messengers: immigrants of color—mostly Asian and Hispanic—whose numbers have greatly increased on campuses since the sixties. These groups, along with African Americans and women, now want access—not just to the corridors of the academy but to its curriculum.

Let's face it: some of the controversy over the canon [of Great Books] and the new multiculturalism has to do with the fact that the complexion of the US—on its campuses and in the country as a whole—is getting darker. In 1960, 94 percent of college students were white. Today almost 20 percent are nonwhite or Hispanic and about 55 percent are women.

It is the confluence of these events—the end of the Cold War and the transformation of the "typical American"—that appears to have stirred up a particularly vocal reaction at this time to the multicultural movement within the academy. . . .

The Response to Multiculturalism

In important ways, hysteria rules the response to multiculturalism. Academic conservatives who defend a canon, tight or loose, sometimes sound as if American universities were fully and finally canonized until the barbarians showed up to smash up the pantheon and install Alice Walker and Toni Morrison in place of the old white men. These conservatives act as if we were floating along in unadulterated canon until sixties radicals came along and muddied the waters. Moreover, the hysterics give the misleading impression that Plato and St. Augustine have been banned.

The tight canonists don't take account either, of the fact that the canon has always been in flux, constantly shifting under our feet. Literary historian Leo Marx made the point that when he was in school it was a fight to get good, gay Walt Whitman into the canon, and to get John Greenleaf Whittier, Henry Wadsworth Longfellow, and James Russell Lowell out.

Still, without doubt there *has* been a dilution of essential modes of critical reasoning, the capacity to write, and a general knowledge of the contours of world history and thought. And this is to be deplored and resisted.

Indeed, there is a side of the academic conservatives argument I agree with. There are a shocking number of students not only in run-of-the-mill segments of higher education but in elite institutions who are amazingly uneducated in history, literature and the fundamentals of logic, who don't know the difference between an argument and an assertion. There *is* a know-nothing mood in some quarters which refuses to understand that the ideas and practices of many a dead white male have been decisive in Western—and therefore world—history.

But the stupidification of our students cannot be blamed simply on shifts in the canon. Cultural illiteracy has crept into our educational process for a variety of reasons. In fact, America's higher illiteracy—to call it by a name Thorstein Veblen might have appreciated—is largely a function of the so-far irresistible force of popular culture as the shaper of popular discourse. By popular discourse, I mean not only the way we speak on the street but the way we speak as presidents and presidential candidates. This is a culture in which "read my lips" or "make my day" constitutes powerful and persuasive speech.

We live in a sound-bite culture, one that has taken anti-elitism as its sacred principle. In the US, to master a vocabulary that is superior to the mediocre is to be guilty of disdain, of scorning democracy. Though conservatives will not be happy to hear about it, this leveling principle has the full force of market capitalism working for it, a force that insists the only standard of value is consumer sovereignty—what people will buy. Since what people will buy are slogans and feel-good pronouncements, it is not surprising that schools and universities have degraded themselves in a frantic pursuit of the lowest common denominator.

The Perils of PC

This said, we must also condemn the bitter intolerance emanating from much of the academic left—steadily more bitter with each passing Republican year as students who feel politically helpless go looking for targets of convenience. The right exaggerates the academic left's power to enforce its prejudices, but is rightly appalled by a widespread self-righteous illiberalism. Academic freedom—the irreducible prerequisite of a democratic society—goes by the board when students at Berkeley and Michigan disrupt classes (whether of a prejudiced anthropologist or a liberal sociologist, respectively). With the long-overdue withering away of Marxism, the academic left has degenerated into a loose aggregation of margins—often cannibalistic, romancing the varieties of otherness, speaking in tongues.

Multiculturalism Prepares Students

Over the past two decades, elementary, middle, and secondary schools and postsecondary institutions have seen efforts to restructure the curriculum in order to represent more adequately the diverse cultures of the student body and the world in which students must eventually function. . . . Comprehensive study of multiple cultures is increasingly recognized as having critical relevance for students who will face a national economy and political structures that grow more globally interdependent and increasingly diverse.

New York State Social Studies Review and Development Committee, *One Nation, Many Peoples: A Declaration of Cultural Interdependence*, June 1991.

In this new interest-group pluralism, the shopping center of identity politics makes a fetish of the virtues of the minority, which, in the end, is not only intellectually stultifying but also politically suicidal. It creates a kind of parochialism in which one is justified in having every interest in difference and no interest in commonality. One's identification with an interest group comes to be the first and final word that opens and terminates one's intellectual curiosity. As soon as I declare I am a Jew, a black, a Hispanic, a woman, a gay, I have no more need to define my point of view.

It is curious and somewhat disturbing that this has become a position on the left since, as Isaiah Berlin has eloquently pointed out in his essays on nationalism, adherents of these views walk head-on into the traditional nationalist trap—a trap that led participants of the German *Sturm und Drang* movement against French cultural imperialism, in the end, to Fascism, brutal irrationalism and the oppression of minorities.

But there is an interesting difference between the German *Sturm und Drang* and our own "Storm and Stress" reaction to monochromatic presentations of history and literature. The Romantics of that period were opposing a French-imposed imperialism. What imperialism is being imposed in the US? Is it the hegemony of Enlightenment ideals of reason and equality, the values of universalism?

If America's multiculturalism means respect for actual difference, we should uphold and encourage this reality against the white-bread, golden-arch version of Disneyland America.

On the other hand, if multiculturalism means there is nothing but difference, then we must do everything we can to disavow it. We cannot condone the creation by the left of separate cultural reservations on which to frolic. There *are* unities—to recognize, to appreciate, deplore, or whatever, but at least to acknowledge. There is America's strange admixture of individualism and conformity. There is the fact of American military, political, cultural, and—still—economic power on a world scale. There are shared myths that cut across tribal lines. We may deplore the ways in which America recognizes itself. Indeed, the Persian Gulf War, the Academy Awards, or the Super Bowl are not high notes in the symphony of civilization, though that is when our culture seems to collectively acknowledge itself. Nonetheless, the US is also a history, an organization of power and an overarching culture. The world is interdependent and America is not simply a sum of marginalities.

Authentic liberals have good reason to worry that the elevation of "difference" to a first principle is undermining everyone's capacity to see, or change, the world as a whole. And those who believe that the idea of the left is an idea of universal interdependence and solidarity—of liberty, equality, fraternity-and-sorority—have reason to mourn the sectarian parochialism of the academic left. To mourn and to organize, so that the right does not, by default, monopolize the legacy of the Enlightenment.

We badly need a careful accounting of the intellectual, social and cultural nature and roots of the new illiteracies and conformities—as well as the academy's high-level efforts to integrate hitherto submerged materials and populations.

It is not a contradiction to say that America has a real culture and also say that this culture is conflicted, fragile, constantly in need of shoring up. The apparent contradiction is only its complexity. In fact, the identity we promote by way of giving lip service to certain ideals about life, liberty and the pursuit of happiness is riddled with contradiction, or at least with tension. Ours is not a relaxed or natural ideology nor was the French Revolution's program of liberty, equality, fraternity. The point is that we can't maximize all values simultaneously.

That is why part of the multicultural program is very important. What is required in a general multicultural program, which is *not* a program for group narcissism, is an understanding of one's own vantage point but also the vantage point of others. If we don't infuse multiculturalism with a respect for the other, all we have is American-style tribalism—a perfect recipe for a home-grown Yugoslavia.

"The bad news is that the radicals are deeply entrenched in academia, and have no plans to go elsewhere."

Political Correctness Is Harmful

Dinesh D'Souza

From his position as a fellow at the American Enterprise Institute, Dinesh D'Souza has emerged as an articulate spokesman for the attack on political correctness, especially in colleges and universities. He has been a frequent guest on television talk shows, and is in demand as a college lecturer. In the following viewpoint, he reviews the origins of the phrase "politically correct," tracing it to its former use by Marxists in the 1950s. He argues that the P.C. phenomenon is a form of political leftism that threatens the freedom of American culture.

As you read, consider the following questions:

1. What does D'Souza say is the greatest obstacle to free speech on college campuses?
2. Why does D'Souza see P.C. continuing to be a controversial issue?

Dinesh D'Souza, "PC So Far." Reprinted from *Commentary*, October 1991, by permission; all rights reserved.

The term "political correctness" seems to have originated in the early part of the century, when it was employed by various species of Marxists to describe and enforce conformity to their preferred ideological positions. Books, films, opinions, even historical events were termed politically correct or politically incorrect depending on whether or not they advanced a particular Marxist view. There is no indication that the revolutionary ideologues and activists of that period spoke of political correctness with any trace of irony or self-mockery.

Eventually the term dropped out of the political lexicon, only to be revived in the early 1980s when it came into use by spokesmen for assorted contemporary ideologies: black consciousness and black power, feminism, homosexual rights, and to a lesser degree pacifism, environmentalism, the counterculture in general. The new *Webster's College Dictionary*, published by Random House, defines political correctness as "marked by or adhering to a typically progressive orthodoxy on issues involving especially race, gender, sexual affinity, or ecology." These days, as most people know, the home of such "typically progressive orthodoxy" is the American university.

Everything Is Political

Like the Stalinists and Trotskyites of an earlier era, contemporary campus activists maintain that "everything is political," and thus to them it seems quite proper to inquire whether classroom lectures, the use of language, and even styles of dress and demeanor reflect a politically correct stance or not. Indeed, many of today's activists are not content with espousing politically correct views themselves, but seek to impose them by force on the new generation of students. So it is that as American society at large is moving toward greater tolerance of heterodox opinion, American universities, ostensibly dedicated to the free traffic of ideas, have been moving in the opposite direction, becoming (in the memorable phrase of Abigail Thernstrom) "islands of repression in a sea of freedom."

More than a hundred universities have instituted censorship codes which typically outlaw racially and sexually "stigmatizing" or offensive speech. Many of the codes are quite broad and elastic: at the University of Connecticut, for example, violations of the ethnic harassment policy, for which the penalty ranges from a reprimand to expulsion, include the "use of derogatory names," "inconsiderate jokes," and even "misdirected laughter" and "conspicuous exclusion from conversation." Although a federal judge struck down as unconstitutional the censorship code in place at the University of Michigan—where a student, hauled up before a disciplinary council for making negative remarks about homosexuality, was recently sentenced to write an apology and to attend sensitivity sessions to transform his unenlightened views—similar regulations are being enforced on many other campuses, and at private colleges they may be immune from First Amendment scrutiny.

© 1993, Ziggy and Friends, Inc. Distributed by Universal Press Syndicate. All rights reserved.

The greatest obstacle to free speech on campus, however, is not the explicit censorship code but a political and social atmosphere in which politically incorrect opinions are discouraged, vilified, and ostracized. Although not a numerical majority, PC activists on campus constitute a kind of "moral majority," enjoying enormous leverage over a predominantly liberal community which is already hypersensitive to hints of racism or bigotry. In several cases, some highly publicized and others relatively unknown, professors who have dissented from PC nostrums have found themselves unemployed, or disgraced by administrative rebuke and sanctions. Many other professors and students have gotten the message: rather than risk being drawn into a vortex of accusations, sensitivity indoctrination, or censure, they simply abstain from articulating unpopular views; they censor themselves. . . .

An Unofficial Ideology

Many mass publications took their first notice of political correctness *per se* in the early 1990s. In "The Rising Hegemony of the Politically Correct" (New York *Times*, October 29, 1990), Richard Bernstein reported a pressure to conform to an "unofficial ideology" among students and faculty of American universities. At a conference in Berkeley, "Political Correctness and Cultural Studies," Bernstein interviewed a number of academics who did not deny that they were engaged in a project of ideological consciousness-raising, but asserted that it was justified by the need to topple "patriarchal hegemony" and the "white male power structure."

Then on December 24, 1990, *Newsweek*, itself a magazine with a "progressive" reputation, surprised everyone with a cover story on today's campus "Thought Police." The article was a parade of horror stories, each showing how professors and students who trespassed on prevailing orthodoxies were made to suffer. Still, the article also implied that university leaders who permitted these excesses were in pursuit of a good cause, and that historical and demographic changes on campus were anyway bound to provoke tensions.

In January 1991, *New York* magazine entered the fray with a vehement blast from John Taylor, "Are You Politically Correct?" Taylor made cruel fun of the PC lexicon, according to which, for instance, pets must be called animal companions and, in one extreme version, short people "vertically challenged." Chuckle we may, wrote Taylor, but many university officials take all this very seriously; an official document at Smith College, for instance, warns students to eschew not only such evils as racism and sexism, but also heterosexism and even lookism—"the belief that appearance is an indicator of a person's value; the construction of a standard for beauty and attractiveness; oppression through stereotypes and generalizations of both those who do not fit that standard and those who do."

While the article in *New York* accurately captured the Star Chamber quality of the political environment on campus, it gave no plausible explanation of who precisely the new McCarthyites were and what they sought to accomplish. Like the *Newsweek* story, however, Taylor's article did help somewhat to delegitimize the PC authoritarians. PC was starting to look uncool.

What followed was an avalanche of critical scrutiny, both in the serious and the popular press, and on television. On February 18, 1991, the *New Republic* published a special issue, "Race on Campus," which included troubling vignettes from several prestigious campuses, an editorial attack on politically correct conformism, and a curious but important article by Irving Howe defending the traditional Western canon. The *New Republic* subsequently published a number of other exposes and essays, including an enthusiastic review of my book, *Illiberal Education*, by the Marxist historian Eugene Genovese, who issued a resounding call for an alliance across the political spectrum to resist PC ideologues and acquiescent administrators. In April 1991, *Time* magazine warned of a "culture of forbidden questions" and a "new intolerance" on campus, while the New York *Times Magazine* published a heavily sarcastic account of the annual convention of the politically correct Modern Language Association, where all the best-attended sessions appeared to focus on sexual deviation, and where classics like Herman Melville's *Moby Dick* fell into the deepest disrepute ("There's not a woman in his book, the plot hinges on unkindness to animals, and the black characters mostly drown by chapter 29").

Where the print media led, television quickly followed. After a talk-show appearance to publicize my book, I was approached by a prominent newscaster who wanted to confide that "all of us here are concerned about the thought police who are roaming our nation's campuses." (This was a much more extreme statement than anything I had or would have uttered—but such is the way of the media.) And on *Good Morning America*, where I was to debate the chancellor of UCLA, the show began with an interview of a pretty young Filipina who despite outstanding grades and extracurricular achievements had been refused admission to Berkeley because, she said, of an anti-Asian quota. When the anchorman kicked off our debate by demanding to know from Chancellor Young what he had to say to the aggrieved young woman, Young's woeful look drove home the degree to which the pendulum had shifted: to the media, university spokesmen, once liberalism's champions, were now its ogres.

A Deafening Silence

How have these spokesmen responded to criticism of the policies they have devised and implemented? So far, with only a couple of exceptions, by a deafening silence.

At first this could perhaps be attributed to the simple bewilderment of a class of people so accustomed to approbation that they had lost even the reflex habit of self-defense. But when weeks and months passed without response or rebuttal, one could only conclude that university leaders were unable to account effectively for their policies, and had decided to lie low until the storm passed—a strikingly pusillanimous posture for those usually so quick to claim a special social prerogative to engage issues of principle.

In any event, the burden of defending PC policies fell at first to political columnists, many of whom had not set foot on a campus for years, and to faculty radicals. In the case of the latter, the results were embarrassing. At the June 1991 conference of the Modern Language Association, for example, the consensus seemed to be that no defense was necessary. The problem was instead that ordinary Americans did not understand the incredible complexities of academia—"It's like trying to reduce a Henry James novel to a telegram," protested Martha Banta of UCLA's English department—or were just plain stupid, "people who don't know the difference between Plato and NATO," in the words of Berkeley sociologist Todd Gitlin, who was head of Students for a Democratic Society in the late 1960s. The only practical suggestion came from Professor Gene Ruoff of the University of Illinois, who urged that radical faculty mount a massive letter-writing and op-ed offensive to explain current academic trends to the general public. But he also conceded the risks of such a campaign; after all, many if not most Americans hold convictions diametrically opposed to those he wished to defend.

By summer, however, it became possible to trace the contours of an argument on behalf of political correctness. The general line, as advanced by Henry Louis Gates, Jr., chairman of Afro-American Studies at Harvard, was that as America becomes a more diverse society, the rules of academic life, heretofore shaped by white males of European origin, will have to be modified in order to reflect multiple voices and interests. Current university policies are based on the recognition that persons of color cannot be expected to homogenize themselves into "an America in cultural white face." A new social compact needs to be negotiated and then institutionalized; while critics of PC may be right to point out a few unfortunate excesses, they have diverted attention from that grand and necessary process.

A similar line was taken by the feminist scholar Catharine Stimpson of Rutgers. In the first place, she maintained, the curriculum has always harbored acknowledged or covert ideological bias. And in the second place, PC activists are not politicizing the curriculum but only attempting to make higher education more accessible, to open closed doors, to promote inclusion. If anything, they should be congratulated for their honesty in unmasking the racial, patriarchal, and heterosexual biases in the so-called great books.

A few have gone farther. On the MacNeil-Lehrer show, Professor Stanley Fish of Duke University asserted that freedom of speech is only one of several competing values worth preserving; sometimes it must be balanced against, or subordinated to, other desiderata. Richard Rosser, president of the Association of Independent Colleges and Universities, while conceding that university codes of censorship may be regrettable, asserted that they are the only way to curb the current campus epidemic of hate speech and racial epithets.

The Destruction of Free Expression

The new academic elite will tell you not to worry, that nothing has happened that need concern parents, trustees, alumni, government or private funding sources. On the issue of enforcing politically correct behavior on campus, for example, they will assure you that the whole thing has been overblown by "conservative" journalists who can't appreciate that the free exchange of ideas must sometimes be curtailed for the higher virtue of protecting the feelings of designated victim groups. . . . What we are facing is nothing less than the destruction of the fundamental premises that underlie both our conception of liberal education and a liberal democratic polity.

Roger Kimball, *The New Criterion*, February 1991.

Mainly, however, the defenders of PC have not sought to justify university policies but to shift the burden to the other side. The threat, they say, is a manufactured one, or at the very least has been greatly exaggerated by conservatives for their own nefarious political ends. "Where's this left-wing reign of terror on campus?" asks the columnist Michael Kinsley in mock-innocence. In a New York *Times* review of my book, Nancy Dye, a dean at Vassar, came close to achieving Orwellian inversion with her charge that the *critics* of PC have framed their case "entirely in polarities," ignoring the "vast middle ground" and mistaking healthy and constructive debate for intimidation. The American Council on Education, which reflects the views of the academic establishment, released a survey of campus administrators most of whom offered a serene and untroubled portrait of the higher-education landscape and failed to see political correctness as a serious problem. The *Village Voice* and the *Nation* have also treated the PC threat as a mythic concoction of the right wing, and Brent Staples of the New York *Times* went so far as to imply that it was a "bogeyman magnified by leftover cold-war hysteria." The darkest pitch of all came from Joel Conarroe, president of the Guggenheim foundation, who suggested that the true goal of critics of PC was to legitimize racism, sexism, and homophobia "as a matter of high principle."

Unfortunately for those who would deny the reality of PC,

however, the facts continue to speak for themselves. As many a politically "incorrect" professor and student can testify, censorship codes are on the books and are being enforced. It has gotten to the point where even some university administrators have begun to admit their concern. Yale president Benno Schmidt, for instance, has warned that nowhere is free speech more endangered today than on the American campus. In his annual report to the Harvard community, outgoing president Derek Bok cited the politicization of the university, primarily along race and gender lines, as one of the greatest perils to liberal education.

If there is any good news, it lies in these isolated voices from within the community of university administrators, bolstered by an un-PC faculty organization like the National Association of Scholars; but it lies even more in the public criticism that has been aired. That criticism has indeed placed PC cadres somewhat on the defensive, a little less quick to ostracize dissenters—especially when there is a chance their activities may be exposed by the media. Even some sensitivity-indoctrination programs now seek "balance" (which usually means allowing one representative of a non-conforming view for every dozen PC advocates). When it comes to the curriculum, although the drive to replace Western-culture requirements with "multicultural" or non-Western programs is already far advanced, it now has to contend with an intellectual opposition, sometimes from emboldened faculty liberals.

But the bad news is that the radicals are deeply entrenched in academia, and have no plans to go elsewhere. In many departments, particularly ones like ethnic and women's studies, faculty ideologues seek to perpetuate their position by hiring only like-minded people, limiting the range of views in some disciplines to what Eugene Genovese terms "a diversity of radical positions." Policies such as racial preference are also thoroughly institutionalized, and have generated vested interests not only among beneficiary groups but also among enforcement bureaucracies.

In short, although the fight against political correctness has so far gone well in the open air of public opinion, the fight on the ground has barely begun.

"On campus, the enemies of diversity are trying to make universities more like fortresses against the siege of . . . uncivilized heathens."

Political Correctness Is Justified

Patricia J. Williams

Beginning with her own experiences of discrimination in the community where she grew up, Patricia J. Williams argues in the following viewpoint that a similar, if more subtle, prejudice pervades American academic life. Williams contends that those who attack advocates of political correctness are actually hoping to roll back hard-won gains achieved by women and minorities. She further contends that the real purpose of the politically correct movement is not censorship, but to develop a sensitivity to the feelings of those historically oppressed. Williams is a professor of law at the University of Wisconsin, and the author of the book, *The Alchemy of Race and Rights*.

As you read, consider the following questions:

1. How was Williams' personal experience linked with those of other oppressed people?
2. What, according to the author, are the two great backlash movements? What does Williams mean by "intellectual blockbusting"?
3. What dilemma does Williams feel that she faces at the present time?

Patricia J. Williams, "Blockbusting the Canon," *Ms.*, September/October 1991. Reprinted by permission of *Ms.* magazine, © 1991.

I am about to turn 40 years old. While I suppose that makes me a Baby Boomer, I have always thought of myself as a Little Rocker: my earliest memories include the integration of the schools in Little Rock, Arkansas, by children just about my age. My life's expanse has marked some of the greatest social movements in this country's history: the civil rights movement, the peace movement, the women's movement, the struggle for the rights of lesbians and gay men, children, the homeless, and the variously abled. My 40 years have traversed oil crises, Motown, Vietnam, liberation from the female necessities of bra, girdle, garters, and straightened hair, and the entire span of Justice Thurgood Marshall's remarkable career.

My age also places me (along with Clarence Thomas) among the very first affirmative action candidates. In the fall of 1969, I entered college as one of 59 blacks; the class ahead of me had only seven. In 1972, I entered law school in a class of only 12 percent women; the class four years later had 25 percent. While the numbers of blacks have suffered real declines with cutbacks in federal tuition support, very few universities in the country have retreated to pre-1970s levels. And while women's presence in universities remains largely ghettoized in many disciplines, most law schools in the country have student populations that are close to 50 percent women. . . .

A Dangerous Crossroads

At the same time, I am convinced we are poised at a dangerous political crossroads that could take us back much more than 40 years. This threat is clear in the right-leaning direction of recent Supreme Court opinions and appointments, the battle over the Civil Rights Bill, the rising rate of bias crimes everywhere, the technologizing of reproduction, and the slick commercialization of "formerly crude" hate mongers from David Duke to Andrew Dice Clay. In academia, this trend has gotten an insidious boost in the right-wing attack on "political correctness." From the *Atlantic Monthly* to *Newsweek* to *This Week with David Brinkley*, there has been a relentless assault on the views of those lumped together hyperbolically as "black activists, militant homosexuals and radical feminists," charging them (us? could that really be me?) with "politicizing" curricula, pushing "intellectual conformity sometimes enforced by intimidation," and turning "whining" into the science of "victimology."

I think that what is going on in the attack on us liberals and Little Rockers is nothing less than *intellectual blockbusting*. I remember when I was little, in the late fifties, two more black families moved into our neighborhood, where for 50 years my family had been the only blacks. I remember the father of my best friend, Cathy, going from house to house, warning the neighbors, like Paul Revere with Chicken Little's brain, that the property values are falling, the values are falling. The area changed overnight. Whites who had seen me born and baked me cookies at Halloween and grown up with my mother fled for their lives. ("We'd have to hold our breath all the time because colored people smell different," said Cathy with some conviction about the pending move. Cathy, who was always a little slow about these things, had difficulty with the notion of me as "colored": "No, you're not" and then, later, "Well, you're different.")

Reprinted by permission: Tribune Media Services.

The mass movement that turned my neighborhood into an "inner city" was part of the first great backlash to the civil rights movement. I think we are now seeing the second great backlash, waged against the hard-won principles of equal opportunity (disguised as a fight about reverse discrimination and "quotas") in the workplace and in universities-as-feeders for the workplace.

On campus, the enemies of diversity are trying to make universities more like fortresses against the siege of those who are perceived to be uncivilized heathens. (Wherever 3 percent or more of us are gathered, it's a siege, I guess.) The cry has been sounded: the standards are falling, the standards are falling.

The story of my inner-city neighborhood would have been vastly different if Cathy and her family had bothered to stick around to get to know the two nice black families who moved in. Similarly, the future of U.S. universities—particularly in the hoped-for global economy—could be a fascinating one if campus communities chose to take advantage of the rich multiculturalism that this society offers. We face a quite disastrous intellectual crisis, however, if our universities persist in the culture-baiting that has brought us the English-only movement, the brazen presumption that any blacks seen on campus don't deserve to be there (in effect, the "Bensonhurstification" of the Ivy

League), and the mounting levels of verbal and physical violence directed against people of color, women, Jews, Arabs, lesbians and gays.

Cultural Stereotypes

Given this, it is all too easy to spend a lot of time being defensive. We've all heard the silly lameness of the retorts into which these attacks box us: "I am too qualified!" "Vote for me but not because I'm a woman!" But it doesn't work. Powerful cultural stereotypes are simply not dispelled by waving your degrees in people's faces. (That's precisely ultraconservative Dinesh D'Souza's whole premise in his much-touted book, *Illiberal Education*: that an Ivy League degree just isn't worth what it used to be now that the riffraff has moved in.)

So enough. Our hardest job in these times is not to forget *why* we (the effete lefty rainbow troublemakers who plot the demise of Dead White Canon-meisters and, god, who Still Read *Ms.* Magazine) are where we are. We cannot forget the strength and comfort of our coalitions, the sacrifice that went into our fragile presence in organizations from grass-roots level to the headiest groves of academe. And we cannot forget that our biggest task in all this is coming together—not merely to overcome the sense of personal diminishment, but to fight *collectively* the persistent devaluation of our intellectual contributions. Recently, for example, I guest-lectured in the class of a constitutional law professor who was teaching disparate impact cases. As I spoke about shifting demographics and white flight, the class grew restless, the students flipping pages of newspapers and otherwise evidencing disrespect. Afterward, the two or three black students congratulated me for speaking so straightforwardly, and for using the words "black" and "white." I later asked the professor, how is it possible to teach cases about racial discrimination without mentioning race? I just teach the neutral principles, he replied; I don't want to risk upsetting the black students. (And yet it was clear that those most upset were the white students.) . . .

The smooth bulwark of "neutral principles" is one way of avoiding the very hard work that moral judgment in any sphere requires, the constant balancing—whether we act as voters, jurors, parents, lawyers, or laypeople—of rules, precepts, principles, and context. I have always thought that developing the ability to engage in such analytical thought is the highest goal of great universities. Yet even this most traditional of educational missions is under attack. "Should [parents] be paying $20,000 a year to have their children sitting there, figuring out how they feel about what they read?" asks James Barber, founder of the neoconservative National Association of Scholars at Duke University. His question underscores the degree to which the right-wing fear of Balkanized campuses is in fact the authoritarian's worst nightmare of a world in which people actually think for themselves. . . .

Learning to See Differences

Learning to see the differences, to understand the pernicious subtlety of what it means to live in a culture of pornography or racism—these are the issues we must be debating in universities. These are the considerations that will best humanize our pedagogy in lasting ways.

As a footnote to this vignette, I daresay it would not come as a great surprise if I mentioned that the real issue got sidetracked by a discussion of the professor's First Amendment rights to academic freedom. The First Amendment, however, has little if anything to do with the real crisis facing our campuses. I'm willing to assume that there's a constitutional right to say anything, anywhere, anytime. But this does not answer the dilemma of how to deal with the concerted propaganda of violence that is subverting any potential for creativity in higher education today.

I want to know, for example, what to do about a black female colleague who went into teaching after a distinguished career as a civil rights litigator. After one year she quit. Among the myriad horror stories she recounts (and that too many of us can recount): A student came to her and told her that there was a bullet with her name on it. At first I thought she was using some kind of awful metaphor, but it turned out that another of her students had actually taken a bullet, carved her name on the side of it, and was showing it to his classmates. (Although the dean of the law school casually promised to mention it to a psychiatrist friend, there was absolutely no institutional response of any sort to this incident.)

Predictably, the ability to mount a campaign of harassment depends on muffling the cries of resistance. In campus politics, this has come in the form of right-wing efforts to disparage the language of resistance: attacks on "sensitivity" as "mental vegetarianism"; charges of sexism, racism, and homophobia as the products of whining immaturity; and victimization as the brewed concoction of practitioners of that dark science, "victimology."

Learning Sensitivity

Yet the ability to be, yes, dammit, *sensitive* to one another is the essence of what distinguishes the joy of multiculturalism or willing assimilation from the oppression of groupthink and totalitarianism. When I was visiting Durham, North Carolina, during the Helms-Gantt election last year [1990], a friend of mine said she wanted me to see something. Without any explanation, she drove me over to the Chapel Hill campus of the University of North Carolina and dragged me to the center of campus. There, right in front of the student union, was a statue entitled "The Student Body." It was a collection of cast bronze figures, slightly smaller than life-size. One was of an apparently white, Mr. Chips-style figure with a satchel of books on his back, pursuing his way. Another was of a young woman of ambiguous racial cast, white or maybe Asian, carrying a violin and some books and earnestly pursuing her way. A third figure was of a young white woman struggling under a load of books stretching from below her waist up to her chin. Then two white figures: a young man holding an open book with one hand; his other arm floated languidly downward, his hand coming to casual rest upon a young woman's buttocks. The young woman leaned into his embrace, her head drooped on her shoulder like a wilted gardenia. In the center of this arrangement was the figure of an obviously black young man. He was dressed in gym shorts and he balanced a basketball on one finger. The last figure was of a solemn-faced young black woman; she walked alone, a solitary book balanced on her head.

A More Representative Educational System

Colleges and universities in the United States have lately begun to serve the majority of Americans better than ever before. Whereas a few short years ago institutions of higher education were exclusive citadels often closed to women, minorities, and the disadvantaged, today efforts are being made to give a far richer diversity of Americans access to a college education. Reforms in the content of the curriculum have also begun to make our classrooms more representative of our nation's diverse peoples and beliefs and to provide a more truthful account of our history and cultural heritage. Much remains to be done, but we can be proud of the progress of democratization in higher education.

Teachers for a Democratic Culture, *Statement of Principles*, 1991.

It turned out that I was about the only one in the state of North Carolina who hadn't heard about this statue. A gift from the class of 1985, it had been the topic of hot debate. Some students, particularly black and feminist students, had complained about the insensitivity of this depiction as representative of the student bod(ies). Other students said the first students were just "being sensitive" (invoked disparagingly, as though numbskulledness were a virtue). At that point the sculptor, a woman, got in on the act and explained that the black male figure was in honor of the athletic prowess of black UNC grads like Michael Jordan, and that the black female figure depicted the grace of black women. The university, meanwhile, congratulated itself publicly on how fruitfully the marketplace of ideas had been stimulated.

As I stood looking at this statue in amazement, I witnessed a piece of the debate-as-education. Two white male students were arguing with a black female student.

"You need to lighten up," said one of the men.

"But . . ." said the black woman.

"Anyway, black women *are* graceful," said the other.

At the end, the black woman walked off in tears, while the white men laughed. There is a litany of questions I have heard raised about scenarios like this: Why should the university "protect" minority students against this sort of thing? Don't they have to learn to deal with it?

Let me pose an alternative set of my own: Why should universities be in the business of putting students in this sort of situation to begin with? Since when is the persistent reduction of black men and all women to their physical traits "educational" of anything? How is it these sorts of ignorant free-for-alls are smiled upon by the same university officials who resist structuring curricula to actually teach the histories of minorities and women?

The Drawbacks to One-on-One

Syndicated columnist Nat Hentoff is very insistent that the solution to the campus multiculturalism struggle is to just talk about it, one-on-one, without institutional sanction or interference. But this solution makes only certain students—those who are most frequently the objects of harassment—the perpetual teachers not merely of their histories, but of their very right just to be students. This is an immense burden, a mountainous presumption of noninclusion that must be constantly addressed and overcome. It keeps us eternally defensive and reactive.

Nor is this issue of legitimacy merely one for students. The respect accorded any teacher is only in small—if essential—part attributable to the knowledge inside one's head. (If that were all, we would have much more respect for street-corner orators, the elderly, and the clear uncensored vision of children.) What makes me a teacher is a force lent to my words by virtue of the collective power of institutional convention. If faculty do not treat women as colleagues, then students will not treat women as members of the faculty.

An example to illustrate the dimension of this problem: A poetry reading at a school where I once taught, a casual event. A white male student in one of my seminars stood up and read a poem attributed to Rudyard Kipling, comparing the relative lustiness of white, brown, yellow, and "nigger" women. In the silence that followed his reading, I asked to go next. I read a short prose poem about my great-great-grandmother having been raped at the age of 11 by her master, my great-great-grandfather. I made no other comment.

The next day, the student went to another faculty member and complained that I seemed unduly upset by his reading; he said he was afraid that I would not be able to grade him objectively, and he would be subjected to the unfairness of my prejudice. The faculty member's response was, "I'm sure you two can work it out."

Now the one thing that this student and I could quickly agree on was that this was a deeply unsatisfactory resolution: in reducing the encounter to one-on-one, this suggestion ignored the extent to which what was going on was (for both of us) a crisis of power, a dislocation of legitimacy. This was no mere difference of individually held opinion, and it could not be resolved at that level. For the university community to act as though it could be was to abandon its function as a player in the moral debate about the propaganda of human devaluation.

The dilemma I face at this moment in the academic world is: If I respond to or open discussion about offensive remarks from students in my classes, I am called "PC" and accused of forcing my opinions down the throats of my students—and of not teaching them the real subject matter. If I respond with no matter what degree of clear, dignified control, I become a militant black female who terrifies "moderate" students. If I follow the prevalent advice of "just ignoring it," then I am perceived as weak, humiliated, ineffectual, a doormat.

It's great to turn the other cheek in the face of fighting words; it's probably even wise to run. But it's not a great way to maintain authority in the classroom—in a society that abhors "wimps" and where "kicking ass" is a patriotic duty. In such a context, "just ignoring" verbal challenges from my law students is a good way to deliver myself into the category of the utterly powerless. If, moreover, my white or male colleagues pursue the same path (student insult, embarrassed pause, the teacher keeps on teaching as though nothing has happened), we have collectively created that peculiar institutional silence that is known as a moral vacuum.

And that, I think, would be the ultimate betrayal of 40 years' worth of hard-won gains.

> *"Liberals and radicals who support 'politically correct' views . . . are endeavoring to defend the rights of women and minorities who have been historically oppressed."*

Attacks on Political Correctness Reveal a Double Standard

Norm Allen

In the following viewpoint, activist and scholar Norm Allen tries to demonstrate that P.C. is largely a myth fabricated by conservatives, to hide their silence or indifference concerning serious problems of racial injustice. He charges them with hypocrisy on the grounds that they are quite vocal when conservatives face criticism, but they remain quiet when victims of racial or sexual prejudice and oppression speak out. Allen is the director of African Americans for Humanism, for whom he edits a newsletter, the *AAH Examiner*; he is also editor of *African-American Humanism: An Anthology.*

As you read, consider the following questions:

1. What examples of the anti-P.C. "double standard" does Allen produce?
2. Does the author favor any form of censorship?
3. What in Allen's view is the real agenda of the right-wing attack on P.C.?

Norm Allen, "Political Correctness and Right-Wing Propaganda," *Freethought History*, No. 5, 1993. Reprinted with permission.

Today there is a debate raging among academics, media pundits, and ordinary citizens throughout the U.S. What is at issue is what is pejoratively referred to as "politically correct" (PC) speech and action. Examples of political correctness include the use of gender-neutral words which acknowledge the existence of women (e.g. "first year student" is used in place of "freshman"), the prohibition of racial slurs, the prohibition of sexist and homophobic speech and writing, etc.

The loudest and most obnoxious opponents of political correctness are mostly reactionary right-wingers with a political agenda of their own. Patrick Buchanan, George Will, William F. Buckley, William Bennett, Jeane Kirkpatrick, and other influential conservatives and neoconservatives have been adamant in their opposition to what they perceive as censorship on the part of school administrators and others in positions of power and authority.

But much to their credit, the anti-PC people have also garnered the support of moderates and paleo-liberals such as Charles Krauthammer, Mike Royko, and Arthur Schlesinger, Jr.

Horror stories about censorship abound in academia and the print media. Indeed, many publications such as *Measure, Heterodoxy,* and *Academic Questions* tend to focus exclusively on the alleged PC threat. For example, on page 3 of the June 1992 issue of *Heterodoxy*, it was reported that Rick Burns, the women's soccer coach at Mount Holyoke College, complained that he could not use the words "girls," "guys," or even "ladies" in reference to players. He was instructed to use the word "women." But when he made reference to a "tall woman," he was reprimanded and instructed to use the words "vertically endowed." Even when he used the word "subs" when referring to substitutes, a player felt that the term was demeaning, and the coach was told to use the word "others." And when he called attention to the outstanding talent of one player, he was accused of ignoring the other players. Many players found his behavior and choice of words to be insulting; and one team member even called for his resignation.

A Double Standard

These well-intentioned but zealous attempts to reduce racism and sexism, and to bring about greater sensitivity and tolerance toward others certainly deserve to be criticized. But the anti-PC grumblers have made it a point to remain silent when the rights of those with whom they disagree have been violated. Following are some examples of the anti-PC double standard:

When irate conservatives demanded that rapper Ice-T's "Cop Killer" record be banned, there was no commotion from the anti-PC mob.

In September 1992, students at Alabama A&M University

charged that controversial rapper Sister Souljah had been prohibited from performing at the school because of a racist statement she is alleged to have made concerning the L.A. riots. The
anti-PC bunch has not commented on this charge.

When the flap over such controversial artists as Robert Mapplethorpe and Andres Serrano (who produced work described as
homo-erotic and blasphemous, respectively) occurred in the
1980s, not only did the anti-PC brigade not complain about the
political correctness movement of the right, but many of them
joined and *led* the right-wing censors.

Similarly, the anti-PC gang led the drive to have Professor
Leonard Jeffries, former African American Studies Department
Chairman at City College of New York (CCNY), removed from
his post. Evidently, Professor Jeffries—an Afrocentrist—did not
espouse the "politically correct" views as far as the right-
wingers were concerned.

An Attack on Everything

The attack on so-called PC, framed as an attack on enforced orthodoxy, one-sided debate, and brainwashing by suspicious academic methodologies is, in fact, an attack on liberal and leftist
ideas generally. Aside from free speech, not a single progressive
concern—women's rights, ecology, minority progress, demilita-
rization, economic transformation—escapes being tarred as an aspect of the PC conspiracy.

Mark M. Hager, *Z Magazine*, April 1992.

Not long ago the Pathfinder Mural which covers the wall of
the Pathfinder Building in New York City was defaced by van-
dals. The mural features portraits of Malcolm X, Karl Marx,
Leon Trotsky, Che Guevara, and other radicals. There was not a
peep to be heard from the anti-PC camp.

But worst of all, the right-wing Oregon Citizens Alliance has
recently proposed an amendment to the Oregon Constitution
which would blatantly discriminate against homosexuals. And
although the anti-PC people are always complaining about "reverse discrimination," they are not complaining about the behavior of these right-wingers in Oregon.

But what other kinds of things *do* the anti-PC people complain
about? They strongly object to the censoring of white
supremacists, male chauvinists, and homophobes. For example,
although they applauded the demotion of Professor Jeffries,
they wholeheartedly endorse City College of New York (CCNY)
professor Michael Levin. While Jeffries has been deemed a

racist, Levin—a white supremacist—is regarded as a sort of hero among the far right. Levin recently mailed out several copies of his thoroughly racist article "Responses to Race Differences in Crime," which appeared in the *Journal of Social Philosophy* XXIII (Spring 1992): 5-29. In the article, Levin argues, among other things, that whites are justified in being afraid of blacks, because a high percentage of blacks tend to be criminals.

In *The Humanist* March/April 1992, Scott Henson and Tom Philpott note in the article "The Right Declares a Culture War," (p. 11), that "Levin has advocated the right of shopkeepers to refuse service to blacks and also thinks whites should have separate cars in the New York subway system."

Levin is strongly supported by the reactionary National Association of Scholars (NAS), probably the most influential anti-PC group, and the publishers of the journal *Academic Questions*. In fact, Henson and Philpott note that Levin served on the NAS board of directors from 1985 to 1989 (page 11).

The highly financed NAS, which was formed primarily to combat political correctness, was once deemed "racist, sexist, and homophobic" by Duke University English professor Stanley Fish. Indeed, in addition to supporting Levin and other white supremacists, Henson and Philpott note that "Joe Horn, a University of Texas at Austin professor who currently sits on the NAS board of directors, has written such articles as "Truth, Gender, and the SAT," published in *Academic Questions*, in which he argues (using virtually no documentation) that gender-based differences in standardized test scores indicate that men are smarter than women.

While censorship of any kind is deplorable, it must be duly noted that liberals and radicals who support "politically correct" views are trying to combat sexual harassment and are endeavoring to defend the rights of women and minorities who have been historically oppressed. But what is one to make of a movement led by tendentious right-wing scholars who primarily defend the rights of bigots and those who espouse ideas which mesh with their own ideologies? The anti-PC people are hardly civil libertarians. It seems that for the right-wingers, this is not so much an issue of free speech as it is an effort to defend the rights of racist, sexist, and homophobic thinkers, and in some cases, to suppress the speech of those with whom they disagree. And ultimately, the right-wingers and their minions want to assure that white, heterosexual males continue to increase their prestige, power and influence everywhere.

"The past is many things, but one thing it is, is irrevocable. A past to your liking is not an entitlement."

Multicultural Education Is Harmful

Thomas Sowell

In this viewpoint, Thomas Sowell address several issues at the core of the movement for more multiculturalism in schools and society. Sowell believes that judgments as to what is better or worse for culture are inevitable in all societies, and, indeed, are necessary. All societies, he says, make such judgments. Sowell is a prominent conservative spokesman in the African-American community. His most recent book is *Inside American Education: The Decline, the Deception, the Dogmas.*

As you read, consider the following questions:

1. What, says the author, was the origin of the movement against slavery?
2. What is Sowell's defense of "dead white males"?
3. What evidence does Sowell produce to support his view that multiculturalism can be a seriously disintegrative force in modern societies?

Thomas Sowell, "Multicultural Instruction," *The American Spectator*, April 1993. Reprinted with permission.

Most of the arguments for so-called "multicultural" education are so flimsy, inconsistent, and downright silly that it is hard to imagine that they would have been taken seriously if they were not backed up by shrill rhetoric, character assassination, and the implied or open threat of organized disruption and violence on campus.

Multiculturalists' Questions

Let us examine the multiculturalists' questions, one by one:
• *Why do we study Western civilization, to the neglect of other civilizations?*

Why is that question asked in English, rather than in some non-Western language? Because English is what we speak. Why do we concern ourselves with the Earth, which is an infinitesimal part of the known universe? Because that is where we live. If we want to understand the cultural and institutional world in which we carry on our daily lives, we need to understand the underlying rationale and the historical evolution of the way of life we have been born into.

None of this has anything to do with whether English is a better language than some other languages. English is in fact more inconsistent and less melodic than French, for example. But we speak English for the same practical reasons that cause people in China to speak Chinese. Attempts to turn this into an invidious comparisons issue miss the fundamental point that (1) languages exist to serve practical purposes and (2) they serve those purposes better, the more people in the same society speak the same language.

Why don't we study other civilizations equally? The most obvious answer is the 24-hour day and the limited number of days we spend in college. It is stretching things very thin to try to cover Western civilization in two semesters. Throw in a couple of other civilizations and you are just kidding yourself that you are educating anybody, when all that you are really doing is teaching them to accept superficiality. Those whose real agenda is propaganda are of course untroubled by such considerations.

Any suggestion that any aspect of Western civilization has been admirable, or better in any way than the corresponding aspect of any other civilization, will of course be loudly denounced as showing bias instead of being "non-judgmental." However, the one thing that no civilization has ever been is non-judgmental. Much of the advancement of the human race has occurred because people made the judgment that some things were not simply different from others, but better. Often this judgment was followed by abandoning one cultural feature and using the other instead.

We use Arabic numerals today, instead of Roman numerals,

even though our civilization derived from Rome, and the Arabs themselves got these numerals from India. Arabic numerals (or Indian numerals) have displaced other numbering systems around the world because they are better—not just different. Paper, printing, and books are today essential aspects of Western civilization, but all three came out of China—and they have displaced parchment, scrolls, and other forms of preserving writings all around the world. Books are not just different, they are better—not just in my opinion, or in the opinion of Western civilization, but in the practice of people around the world who have had an opportunity to make the comparison. Firearms have likewise displaced bows and arrows wherever the two have come into competition.

Signe Wilkinson, by permission of Cartoonists & Writers Syndicate.

Many of those who talk "non-judgmental" rhetoric out of one side of their mouths are quick to condemn the evils of "our society" out of the other side. Worse, they condemn American society or Western civilization for sins that are the curse of the human race all across the planet. Indeed, they condemn the West for sins that are worse in many non-Western societies.

Perhaps the classic case is slavery. The widespread revulsion which this hideous institution inspires today was largely confined to Western civilization a century ago, and a century before that was largely confined to a portion of British society. No one seems interested in the epic story of how this curse that covered the globe and endured for thousands of years was finally gotten rid of. It was gotten rid of by the West—not only in Western societies but in other societies conquered, controlled, or pressured by the West.

The resistance put up by Africans, Asians, and Arabs was monumental in defense of slavery, and lasted for more than a century. Only the overwhelming military power of the West enabled it to prevail on this issue, and only the moral outrage of Western peoples kept their governments' feet to the fire politically to maintain the pressure against slavery around the world. Of course, this is not the kind of story that appeals to the multiculturalists. If it had been the other way around—if Asian or African imperialists had stamped out slavery in Europe—it would still be celebrated, in story and song, on campuses across America.

• *Why are the traditional classics of Western civilization written by dead white males?*

Take it a step at a time. They are written by dead people for two reasons: First, there are more dead people than living people. Second, a classic is not something that is hot at the moment but something that survives the test of time. There may be things written today that will survive to become classics, but we won't be here when that happens. The things we know are classics were almost by definition written by dead people.

Why were they white? Do we ask why the great classics of China were written by people who were Chinese? If we found that the great classics of China were written by Swedes, wouldn't we wonder what the hell was going on?

Should there be any mystery as to why they were written by males? Is anyone so utterly ignorant of history that they do not know that females had more than enough other work to keep them busy for most of the history of the human race? Maybe men should have shared some of that work. But history is what happened, not what we wish had happened. If most of the people who were educated were male—as they have been throughout history, and even are today in some societies—then most of the people who leave the kind of written material left by educated people will be men. You don't get great mathematical discoveries from people who were never taught algebra.

The Oppressed and Under-Represented

Much the same reasoning applies to other groups considered to be (1) oppressed and (2) "under-represented" among those whose historic achievements and contributions are recognized. But how can a people's achievements be unaffected by their oppression? One of the many reasons to be against oppression is that it keeps people from achieving all that they could have

107

achieved if they had been treated more decently. To proclaim oppression and still expect to find the oppressed equally represented among those with historic achievements and contributions is almost a contradiction in terms.

The past is many things, but one thing it is, is irrevocable. A past to your liking is not an entitlement.

• *Don't we need multiculturalism to get people to understand each other and get along with each other?*

Since this is an empirical question, you would expect people to seek an empirical answer, yet most of those who talk this way seem content to treat the matter as axiomatic. But is there any evidence that colleges that have gone whole hog into multiculturalism have better relations among the various groups on campus? Or is it precisely on such campuses that separatism and hostility are worse than on campuses that have not gone in for the multicultural craze?

You want to see multiculturalism in action? Look at Yugoslavia, at Lebanon, at Sri Lanka, at Northern Ireland, at Azerbaijan, or wherever else group "identity" has been hyped. There is no point in the multiculturalists' saying that this is not what they have in mind. You might as well open the floodgates and then say that you don't mean for people to drown. Once you have opened the floodgates, you can't tell the water where to go.

• *How are we to be part of the global economy, or engage in all sorts of other international activities, without being multicultural?*

Ask the Japanese. They are one of the most insular and self-complacent peoples on Earth today. Yet they dominate international markets, international finance, international scientific and technological advances, and send armies of tourists around the world. This is not a defense of insularity or of the Japanese. It is simply a plain statement of fact that contradicts one of the many lofty and arbitrary dogmas of multiculturalism.

"Integrating African Americans into the mainstream will benefit everyone in the long run, and is the only practical solution to racism."

Multicultural Education Is Helpful

William Sierichs Jr.

A central motivation for multiculturalism, William Sierichs Jr. contends in the following viewpoint, is to combat all forms of racism, which presently impedes human progress. Sierichs draws on some fundamental achievements of widely differing civilizations to support the idea that multiculturalism is simply based on the truth about history. Sierichs is a member of the Shreveport Humanists in Shreveport, Louisiana.

As you read, consider the following questions:

1. What valuable achievements, according to Sierichs, have emerged from non-Western civilizations?
2. What valuable achievements does Sierichs believe have been produced by European civilization?
3. Have Europeans been the only violent or racist societies, according to the author?

From William Sierichs Jr., "Humanism, Racism, and Multiculturalism," parts 2 and 3, African Americans for Humanism *Examiner*, Summer and Fall 1992. Reprinted with permission.

Much of the debate over multiculturalism derives from racial viewpoints. When conservatives argue for a "Western culture" education, their idea implicitly considers "Western," i.e., "White" culture to be so much superior that other cultures have little of value worth studying.

The multiculturalists' argument basically adopts the premise that all cultures have something valuable to say, and that a "Western" culture-only education is too limited, and further-more, helps to perpetuate racism by implicitly denigrating all non-White cultures. . . .

Traditional Education

Traditional education centered around "Western" culture. Stu-dents had to read specific works written by various European writers, beginning with Homer (who actually was an Asian Greek, not a mainland European), continuing through the Clas-sical Greeks on down to Europeans and Americans.

The Bible is also generally considered a necessary part of the education, even though it appeared in the Middle East, outside of the mainstream of European history.

So what does this leave out? A few examples:

1) Much of our basic morality is found in Egyptian and Mesopotamian literature. The moral ideas of the Ten Command-ments first appear among the Egyptians as early as the third millennium (B.C.E.) [Before the Common Era], and in at least one Assyrian text. Reading the Bible without having read a com-prehensive selection of Bronze Age Egyptian and Mesopotamian literature is like reading an anthology of twentieth-century American literature while being ignorant of everything written before 1900 C.E.

2) Writing itself was a non-European invention. The alphabet, an important concept for sophisticated communications, first appears among the Bronze Age Canaanites, possibly inspired by Egyptian hieratic, a cursive, shorthand form of hieroglyphs. When we refer to the "Greek alphabet," we actually mean the Canaanite alphabet.

3) The Pythagorean theorem is taught in school, yet Pythago-ras only offered a formal proof for a mathematical formula that was taught at least 1,000 years earlier in Mesopotamia and prob-ably Egypt as well.

4) Modern math would be impossible if we had to use the Ro-man numeral system. Place-value math systems were invented at least three times in history, but never in Europe.

The Babylonians and Mayan Indians all had place-value math systems. The base-ten version we use comes from Hindu mathe-maticians, reaching Europe by way of the Islamic Arabs, who devised our numbers.

These are but a few of the important ideas that appeared outside of the Classical Greece-to-modern Europe civilization axis.

A major part of the multiculturalism effort comes from African Americans. Various scholars have shown that racially motivated European scholars deliberately ignored or downplayed the roles of Africans in history. Blacks are trying to recover their heritage, both for their own benefit and to correct the historical record.

One example: I have seen a Ku Klux Klan pamphlet that claims that Blacks never had a great civilization. That can be said only if one refuses to call Ancient Egypt "great."

Breaking the Barriers

Multiculturalism has a separatist current (if I'm Latino and you're not, you can't use my secret handshake), and some of it is, alas, necessary for survival—literally, in some streets, culturally, in some salons. It also has an integrationist current. And that means enlarging the scope of culture by breaking down the artificial barriers erected by chauvinism.

Enrique Fernández, *The Village Voice*, June 18, 1991.

The original Egyptian civilization sprang up among an African people who would certainly be classified as "Black" under today's racial divisions. And from that African people 5,000 years ago developed one of history's seminal cultures. Their achievements ranged from monumental architecture to delicate arts and crafts, to a literature that includes ebullient hymns, fairy tales, and delicious love poems, and to an early basis for later science and technology.

The treasures of Tutankhamen open a window on the beauty and virtuosity of Egyptian art. Yet if the young pharaoh had somehow come to life in 1922, he would have been barred from all of the "Whites only" facilities of America.

His dark skin and the Negroid features of his face would have marked him in a racist society. A full history of Ancient Egypt knocks the Klan's claim into the dustbin of historical garbage, and also provides an excellent argument for multiculturalism. The narrow focus of the traditional "Western" education can leave the recipient ignorant of too much and imbued with a false pride that arrogantly assumes that what he or she has studied is all that is worth studying.

A broader education is lethal both to cultural arrogance and the racism that it helps engender. . . .

Scholarship is not simply a matter of making bold claims; it requires a careful effort at accuracy, a caution when the evidence is weak or dubious, and a constant attention to credibility.

The extreme claims of some historical revisionists harm the progress of multiculturalism. Consider these distortions:

1) Europeans were not demonstrably more vicious, aggressive, or bigoted than other peoples. Asia, Africa and the Americas all offer numerous examples of violence, imperialism, and ethnic intolerance. These, tragically, are humanity's common heritage.

Even the European's aggression toward the American Indians has a parallel from their own history. From the 5th century C.E. (Common Era) to the 13th century, Europe was invaded repeatedly from the Asian steppes by Huns, Avars, Magyars, Bulgars and Mongols. While the Goths originated in northern Europe, to Romanized Europeans they were quite alien intruders.

In the 8th century, an Islamic army of Arabs and Africans conquered Spain and raided southern France. Only the fortunes of war prevented Arabs and Africans from overrunning Europe. Islamic armies repeatedly assailed the Christian Byzantine empire; and despite theological differences, the Roman Catholics of Western Europe regarded Constantinople as a bastion against an alien enemy. Constantinople's fall in 1453, and subsequent invasions by the Turks (an East Asian people who originally displaced the inhabitants of Anatolia) as far as Vienna, were traumatic for Europeans. Many Europeans spent their lives in slavery in Africa or Asia during these conflicts.

In short, the events of 1492, when the last Arab-African stronghold of Granada fell and when Columbus voyaged, could be viewed as part of a European counterattack after centuries of outside assaults. It was the American Indians' misfortune that they were too weak politically and technologically to resist; while many Africans paid for Islam's attacks on Europe. This is as plausible a view as the "Europeans as evil imperialists" claims of some multiculturalists.

2) Bigotry, also, is not unique to Western societies. Racism was a major factor in Japan's brutal treatment of non-Japanese peoples—including Europeans and Americans—in the 1930s and in World War II. A seeming revival of that racism, as seen in the contemptuous remarks of Japanese politicians toward Blacks and other minorities, has been noted in recent years.

The Chinese were long contemptuous toward "barbarians" who did not live within the borders of the Middle Kingdom—a term implying that China was the middle of the world. Not long ago, race riots by Chinese drove African students from some colleges in China.

Effects of Tribal Loyalties

Although racism in the modern sense was not found among Africans or American Indians, tribal loyalties created sharp divisions among the peoples of Africa and the Americas. European intervention exacerbated but did not create the tribal struggles in Africa. The Zulu conquests under Shaka Zulu, with the sometimes ruthless slaughter of hostile tribes, occurred before significant European contact, for example. The American Indians' tribal wars could be quite fierce. Again, Europeans made the slaughter worse by supplying guns, but this only allowed the better-armed tribes to win crushing victories in longstanding feuds.

Early European explorers chronicled the Indians' torture of captives and the pitiful plight of refugees who were driven from their homes, often to die of starvation or exposure.

The famed Aztecs were essentially a tribe of "barbarians" from western Mexico who conquered and ruthlessly dominated the older civilizations of central Mexico. Cortez's invasion sparked a rebellion among some of the oppressed Mexican tribes, and it was this civil war within the Aztecs' empire, along with an epidemic of European-derived smallpox among the Aztecs, that gave Cortez his victory. Without his Indian allies, Cortez might well have found himself the guest of honor at an Aztec sacrificial ceremony. . . .

3) If Europeans' contributions to civilization were reduced to their essentials, they could probably be summarized as these, perhaps two of the most important ideas in history: the scientific method and constitutional democracy.

The scientific method requires a combination of observation, experimentation, cautious theorizing, testing of results and rigorous scrutiny of claims. It is the only proven method for understanding the natural world, and secular humanism is one of its many offspring. The scientific method replaces, and repudiates, all the many forms of superstition that people have employed traditionally in dealing with nature, being ignorant of the natural laws that underlie the universe.

Constitutional democracy differs from Classical Greek democracy and Roman republicanism in that it incorporates that famous balance of powers and also guarantees rights to all citizens, no matter how unpopular the individual may be. Greek democracy was always vulnerable to tyranny by the majority; the Romans had no defense against a skilled leader accumulating overwhelming power in his hands.

Americans, particularly Madison and Jefferson, noted these hazards and made provisions against them. The architects of the French and Russian revolutions ignored history, and the French and Russians both paid terrible prices for their arrogance. Similarly, one-party governments in various countries today lead their peoples down the same cruel paths as ruined the Greeks and Romans.

Any society which wants to avoid the fate of non-democratic

systems must study the course of Western history and culture to understand how and why constitutional democracy developed, and why the scientific method is vital.

4) The United States originated as a British colony. To understand the history of the U.S.—both the good and the bad—and its culture, an education in Western culture is vital. The history, literature and philosophy of the West are an essential part of an American education. In rewriting history texts, and in revising reading lists for humanities courses, many of the traditional texts must be retained for the benefit of Americans of all backgrounds.

Although many Americans are of European descent, they are not Europeans. Subtle but distinct differences divide the New World from the Old. Similarly, Americans of African descent are not Africans. While the intolerance of some Whites may drive many Blacks to a new self-segregation, the mingling of various cultures in the U.S. makes it impossible for any group to separate itself indefinitely. Integrating African Americans into the mainstream will benefit everyone in the long run, and is the only practical solution to racism. As a wise man once said, "A house divided cannot stand."

If the West is guilty of bigotry, slavery, imperialism and repression of non-Western cultures, it also has produced eloquent defenses of tolerance, freedom and diversity. The assault on slavery worldwide and the recovery of lost history, including Egypt's and Mesopotamia's, through archaeology, were byproducts of constitutional democracy and the scientific method.

There is much the world can learn from the West. Rejecting Western culture is a form of intellectual self-mutilation as severe as rejecting multiculturalism.

Secular humanism prides itself on a respect for diverse viewpoints and for tolerance of conflicting or unpopular opinions. It should be noted that *Free Inquiry* magazine printed articles on *Black Athena* and Afrocentrism a year-and-a-half before they were taken up by some of the major media.

This is consistent with secular humanism, which is directed to—and in ideal terms covers—all humanity. "We hold these truths to be self-evident, that all men are created equal." If we believe in this famous humanist creed (adjusted to a non-sexist form), then we must accept that all people on this planet deserve an equal role in their societies and are capable of escaping the bonds of tyrannical ideas that have restricted humanity over the centuries.

Racism and ethnocentrism are two such notions, as much a threat to civilization as religion. Humanists cannot afford to ignore any of these bigotries, because a threat to one person's rights is a threat to everyone's rights. That is part of the message we can give, both to the world and to those peoples traditionally targeted by bigots.

Periodical Bibliography

The following articles have been selected to supplement the diverse views presented in this chapter.

Molefi Kete Asante
"Multiculturalism: An Exchange," *American Scholar*, Spring 1991.

Ward Churchill
"Fantasies of the Master Race: Categories of Stereotyping of American Indians in Film," *Book Forum*, Vol. 3, No. 3, 1981.

Midge Decter
"E Pluribus Nihil: Multiculturalism and Black Children," *Commentary*, September 1991.

Troy Duster
"They're Taking Over! And Other Myths About Race on Campus," *Mother Jones*, September/October 1991.

Barbara Ehrenreich
"What Campus Radicals?" *Harper's*, December 1991.

Chester E. Finn Jr.
"The Campus: An Island of Repression in a Sea of Freedom," *Commentary*, September 1989.

Henry Louis Gates Jr.
"Whose Canon Is It, Anyway?" *New York Times Book Review*, February 26, 1989.

The Humanist
"Democracy and Multiculturalism," March/April 1992.

Roger Kimball
"A Multicultural Morass," *The Wall Street Journal*, February 20, 1992.

Brenda Mitchell-Powell
"Color Me Multi-Cultural," *Multicultural Review*, October 1992.

New Perspectives Quarterly
"Too Open-Minded for Our Own Good?" Winter 1988.

The New Republic
"Race on Campus," February 18, 1991.

Newsweek
"Was Cleopatra Black?" September 23, 1991.

Ruth Perry
"A Short History of the Term Politically Correct," *Women's Review of Books*, February 1992.

Diane Ravich
"Multiculturalism: E Pluribus Plures," *American Scholar*, Summer 1990.

Lillian S. Robinson
"What Culture Should Mean," *The Nation*, September 25, 1989.

Linda Salamon
"When Nobody Reasons Together," *New York Times Book Review*, April 11, 1993.

John Searle
"The Storm Over the University," *New York Review of Books*, December 6, 1990.

Wilcomb E. Washburn
"Liberalism Versus Free Speech," *National Review*, September 30, 1988.

George F. Will
"The Liberals Favor Censorship of Speech," *Conservative Chronicle*, November 15, 1988.

C. Vann Woodward
"Freedom and the University," *New York Review of Books*, July 18, 1991.

Is American Culture Decadent?

**CULTURE
WARS**

Chapter Preface

"It's Morning in America," proclaimed the television advertising campaign for Ronald Reagan in 1984, portraying a clean pleasant neighborhood of happy people going to work and school. This expression of free enterprise optimism and national renewal was appealing and effective. Yet, by the latter part of the eighties, our society faced critical problems of chronic unemployment, drug abuse, infrastructure decay, and violent crime. In such an uneasy, tense atmosphere, many people charged that American culture is leading to this decay, pushing us near national collapse.

No human society is ever static, going through cycles of birth, growth, maturity, and, perhaps, demise. Since Edward Gibbon's classic *Decline and Fall of the Roman Empire*, written in the late eighteenth century, modern historians have possessed tools for evaluating the process of decadence. With calm, majestic prose, Gibbon explained how a combination of moral corruption, love of luxury, and barbarian invasions led to the utter collapse of the once vast political and economic power of Rome. The deplorable advance of immorality—decadence—led inevitably to a loss of authority and social control. In the twentieth century, several great empires, including those of Russia, Germany, and Britain have collapsed for some of these same reasons.

Americans, for most of their history, have been an optimistic people, believing that evolving democratic institutions and extensive natural resources would prevent the nation's decline of power in the world. But now many contemporary analysts and writers are discussing the question of whether the United States is now undergoing a similar process of decadence. But how exactly do we decide if a society or a culture is decadent? In former times, kissing or "close dancing" were widely viewed as unacceptable. Yet today, that would seem mild indeed to most people. How do we determine that things are worsening? The popularity of such phenomena as rock and rap music—with the prevalence of sexual imagery and profane language—is viewed by many as proof of America's decline, whereas others conclude that this music reflects the raw, powerful reality of life for young and minority people today. The authors in this chapter debate whether America is becoming decadent, and whether it is necessary to try to reverse our cultural directions.

"Rock music has one appeal only, a barbaric appeal, to sexual desire . . . undeveloped and untutored."

Rock Music Has Harmed American Youth

Allan Bloom

As a professor of philosophy who translated Plato's *Republic*, Allan Bloom has used the concepts found in classical culture to help explain what is happening in American society today. In the following viewpoint, he explains Plato's theory of good music, which prefers stately and dignified "march" type music to lascivious and sensual "dances." Bloom contends that present-day rock music arises from the latter tradition, and that it caters to shallow spontaneity and adolescent sexual fantasies. Because rock fixates on such aims, says Bloom, it cannot lead young people toward reason and maturity in their lives.

As you read, consider the following questions:

1. What does the author mean when he says rock music is "unquestioned and unproblematic"?
2. How, according to Bloom, does Plato's theory about music being "the barbarous expression of the soul" explain the nature of rock music?
3. Why does Bloom argue that rock music is "an art form directed exclusively to children"?

From *The Closing of the American Mind* by Allan Bloom. Copyright © 1987 by Allan Bloom. Reprinted by permission of Simon & Schuster.

Though students do not have books, they most emphatically do have music. Nothing is more singular about this generation than its addiction to music. This is the age of music and the states of soul that accompany it. . . . Today, a very large proportion of young people between the ages of ten and twenty live for music. It is their passion; nothing else excites them as it does; they cannot take seriously anything alien to music. When they are in school and with their families, they are longing to plug themselves back into their music. Nothing surrounding them—school, family, church—has anything to do with their musical world. At best that ordinary life is neutral, but mostly it is an impediment, drained of vital content, even a thing to be rebelled against. . . . It is available twenty-four hours a day, everywhere. There is the stereo in the home, in the car; there are concerts; there are music videos, with special channels exclusively devoted to them, on the air nonstop; there are the Walkmans so that no place—not public transportation, not the library—prevents students from communing with the Muse, even while studying. And, above all, the musical soil has become tropically rich. No need to wait for one unpredictable genius. Now there are many geniuses, producing all the time, two new ones rising to take the place of every fallen hero. There is no dearth of the new and the startling. . . .

Rock music is as unquestioned and unproblematic as the air the students breathe, and very few have any acquaintance at all with classical music. This is a constant surprise to me. And one of the strange aspects of my relations with good students I come to know well is that I frequently introduce them to Mozart. This is a pleasure for me, inasmuch as it is always pleasant to give people gifts that please them. It is interesting to see whether and in what ways their studies are complemented by such music. But this is something utterly new to me as a teacher; formerly my students usually knew much more classical music than I did. . . .

Plato and Music

Symptomatic of this change is how seriously students now take the famous passages on musical education in Plato's *Republic*. In the past, students, good liberals that they always are, were indignant at the censorship of poetry, as a threat to free inquiry. But they were really thinking of science and politics. They hardly paid attention to the discussion of music itself and, to the extent that they even thought about it, were really puzzled by Plato's devoting time to rhythm and melody in a serious treatise on political philosophy. Their experience of music was as an entertainment, a matter of indifference to political and moral life. Students today, on the contrary, know exactly why Plato takes music so seriously. They know it affects life very profoundly and are indignant because Plato seems to want to rob them of their most intimate pleasure. They are drawn into argument with Plato about the experience of music, and the dispute centers on how to evaluate it and deal with it. This encounter not only helps to illuminate the phenomenon of contemporary music, but also provides a model of how contemporary students can profitably engage with a classic text. The very fact of their fury shows how much Plato threatens what is dear and intimate to them. They are little able to defend their experience, which had seemed unquestionable until questioned, and it is most resistant to cool analysis. Yet if a student can—and this is most difficult and unusual—draw back, get a critical distance on what he clings to, come to doubt the ultimate value of what he loves, he has taken the first and most difficult step toward the philosophic conversion. Indignation is the soul's defense against the wound of doubt about its own; it reorders the cosmos to support the justice of its cause. It justifies putting Socrates to death. Recognizing indignation for what it is constitutes knowledge of the soul, and is thus an experience more philosophic than the study of mathematics. It is Plato's teaching that music, by its nature, encompasses all that is today most resistant to philosophy. So it may well be that through the thicket of our greatest corruption runs the path to awareness of the oldest truths.

Plato's teaching about music is, put simply, that rhythm and melody, accompanied by dance, are the barbarous expression of the soul. Barbarous, not animal. Music is the medium of the *human* soul in its most ecstatic condition of wonder and terror. Nietzsche, who in large measure agrees with Plato's analysis, says in *The Birth of Tragedy* (not to be forgotten is the rest of the title, *Out of the Spirit of Music*) that a mixture of cruelty and coarse sensuality characterized this state, which of course was religious, in the service of gods. Music is the soul's primitive and primary speech and it is *alogon*, without articulate speech or reason. It is not only not reasonable, it is hostile to reason. Even when articulate speech is added, it is utterly subordinate to and determined by the music and the passions it expresses.

Civilization or, to say the same thing, education is the taming or domestication of the soul's raw passions—not suppressing or excising them, which would deprive the soul of its energy—but forming and informing them as art. The goal of harmonizing the enthusiastic part of the soul with what develops later, the rational part, is perhaps impossible to attain. But without it, man can never be whole. Music, or poetry, which is what music becomes as reason emerges, always involves a delicate balance between passion and reason, and, even in its highest and most developed forms—religious, warlike and erotic—that balance is always tipped, if ever so slightly, toward the passionate. Music, as everyone experiences, provides an unquestionable justification and a fulfilling pleasure for the activities it accompanies: the soldier who hears the marching band is enthralled and reassured; the religious man is exalted in his prayer by the sound of the organ in the church; and the lover is carried away and his conscience stilled by the romantic guitar. Armed with music, man can damn rational doubt. Out of the music emerge the gods that suit it, and they educate men by their example and their commandments. . . .

A Barbaric Appeal

Rock music . . . has risen to its current heights in the education of the young on the ashes of classical music, and in an atmosphere in which there is no intellectual resistance to attempts to tap the rawest passions. Modern-day rationalists, such as economists, are indifferent to it and what it represents. The irrationalists are all for it. There is no need to fear that "the blond beasts" are going to come forth from the bland souls of our adolescents. But rock music has one appeal only, a barbaric appeal, to sexual desire—not love, not *eros*, but sexual desire undeveloped and untutored. It acknowledges the first emanations of children's emerging sensuality and addresses them seriously, eliciting them and legitimating them, not as little sprouts that must be carefully tended in order to grow into gorgeous flowers, but as the real thing. Rock gives children, on a silver platter, with all the public authority of the entertainment industry, everything their parents always used to tell them they had to wait for until they grew up and would understand later.

Young people know that rock has the beat of sexual intercourse. That is why Ravel's *Bolero* is the one piece of classical music that is commonly known and liked by them. In alliance with some real art and a lot of pseudo-art, an enormous industry cultivates the taste for the orgiastic state of feeling connected with sex, providing a constant flood of fresh material for voracious appetites. Never was there an art form directed so exclusively to children.

Ministering to and according with the arousing and cathartic music, the lyrics celebrate puppy love as well as polymorphous attractions, and fortify them against traditional ridicule and shame. The words implicitly and explicitly describe bodily acts that satisfy sexual desire and treat them as its only natural and routine culmination for children who do not yet have the slightest imagination of love, marriage or family. This has a much more powerful effect than does pornography on youngsters, who have no need to watch others do grossly what they can so easily do themselves. Voyeurism is for old perverts; active sexual relations are for the young. All they need is encouragement. . . .

Picture a thirteen-year-old boy sitting in the living room of his family home doing his math assignment while wearing his Walkman headphones or watching MTV. He enjoys the liberties hard won over centuries by the alliance of philosophic genius and political heroism, consecrated by the blood of martyrs; he is provided with comfort and leisure by the most productive economy ever known to mankind; science has penetrated the secrets of nature in order to provide him with the marvelous, lifelike electronic sound and image reproduction he is enjoying. And in what does progress culminate? A pubescent child whose body throbs with orgasmic rhythms; whose feelings are made articulate in hymns to the joys of onanism or the killing of parents; whose ambition is to win fame and wealth in imitating the drag-queen who makes the music. In short, life is made into a nonstop, commercially prepackaged masturbational fantasy. . . .

Music's Effect on Behavior

Common sense tells us that, just as the great music of Handel, Hayden, Bach, Beethoven, Mozart, Vivaldi and Wagner can educate, enlighten, and inspire, the music and lyrics of all too many rock songs can corrupt by glamorizing and encouraging self- and socially-destructive behavior.

Haven Bradford Gow, *Conservative Review*, October 1990.

My concern here is not with the moral effects of this music— whether it leads to sex, violence or drugs. The issue here is its effect on education, and I believe it ruins the imagination of young people and makes it very difficult for them to have a passionate relationship to the art and thought that are the substance of liberal education. The first sensuous experiences are decisive in determining the taste for the whole of life, and they are the link between the animal and spiritual in us. The period of nascent sensuality has always been used for sublimation, in the sense of making sublime, for attaching youthful inclinations and longings to music, pictures and stories that provide the transition to the fulfillment of the human duties and the enjoyment of the human pleasures. Doris Lessing, speaking of Greek sculpture, said "beautiful men made beautiful statues, and the city had beautiful statues in part to thank for beautiful citizens." This formula encapsulates the fundamental principle of the esthetic education of man. Young men and women were attracted by the beauty of heroes whose very bodies expressed their nobility. The deeper understanding of the meaning of nobility comes later, but is prepared for by the sensuous experience and is actually contained in it. What the senses long for as well as what reason later sees as good are thereby not at tension with one another. Education is not sermonizing to children against their instincts and pleasures, but providing a natural continuity between what they feel and what they can and should be. But this is a lost art. Now we have come to exactly the opposite point. Rock music encourages passions and provides models that have no relation to any life the young people who go to universities can possibly lead, or to the kinds of admiration encouraged by liberal studies. Without the cooperation of the sentiments, anything other than technical education is a dead letter.

Rock music provides premature ecstasy and, in this respect, is like the drugs with which it is allied. It artificially induces the exaltation naturally attached to the completion of the greatest endeavors—victory in a just war, consummated love, artistic creation, religious devotion and discovery of the truth. Without effort, without talent, without virtue, without exercise of the faculties, anyone and everyone is accorded the equal right to the enjoyment of their fruits. In my experience, students who have had a serious fling with drugs—and gotten over it—find it difficult to have enthusiasms or great expectations. It is as though the color has been drained out of their lives and they see everything in black and white. The pleasure they experienced in the beginning was so intense that they no longer look for it at the end, or as the end. They may function perfectly well, but dryly, routinely. Their energy has been sapped, and they do not expect their life's activity to produce anything but a living, whereas liberal education is supposed to encourage the belief that the good life is the pleasant life and that the best life is the most pleasant life. I suspect that the rock addiction, particularly in the absence of strong counterattractions, has an effect similar to that of drugs. The students will get over this music, or at least the exclusive passion for it. But they will do so in the same way Freud says that men accept the reality principle—as something harsh, grim and essentially unattractive, a mere necessity. These students will assiduously study economics or the professions and the Michael Jackson costume will slip off to reveal a Brooks Brothers suit beneath. They will want to get ahead and live comfortably. But this life is as empty and false as the one they left behind. The choice is not between quick fixes and dull calculation. This is what liberal education is meant to show them. But as long as they have the Walkman on, they cannot hear what the great tradition has to say. And, after its prolonged use, when they take it off, they find they are deaf.

"For rock to move forward as an art form, our musicians must be given the opportunity for spiritual development."

Rock Music Has Liberated American Youth

Camille Paglia

In 1990, Yale University Press published *Sexual Personae* by Camille Paglia, then a teacher at an art school in Philadelphia. Through a combination of circumstances, Paglia was soon launched into a career as a media personality. Her acerbic, lively style and outspoken defense of rock music, popular culture, prostitution, homosexuality and "decadent" art in general attracted wide attention and intense controversy. In the following viewpoint, Paglia defends rock music as an authentic expression of modern feelings and emotions.

As you read, consider the following questions:

1. Why, according to Paglia, is rock music democratic? Does this contradict its commercial aspects?
2. Why does Paglia contend that the rock concert format has "become progressively less conducive to music-making"?
3. What does the author believe rock musicians should do concerning education?

Camille Paglia, "Rock as Art," *The New York Times*, April 16, 1992. Copyright © 1992 by The New York Times Company. Reprinted by permission.

Rock is eating its young. Rock musicians are America's most wasted natural resource.

Popular music and film are the two great art forms of the twentieth century. In the past twenty-five years, cinema has gained academic prestige. Film courses are now a standard part of the college curriculum and grants are routinely available to noncommercial directors.

But rock music has yet to win the respect it deserves as the authentic voice of our time. Where rock goes, democracy follows. The dark poetry and surging Dionysian rhythms of rock have transformed the consciousness and permanently altered the sensoriums of two generations of Americans born after World War Two.

Rock music should not be left to the Darwinian laws of the marketplace. This natively American art form deserves national support. Foundations, corporations and Federal and state agencies that award grants in the arts should take rock musicians as seriously as composers and sculptors. Colleges and universities should designate special scholarships for talented rock musicians. Performers who have made fortunes out of rock are ethically obligated to finance such scholarships or to underwrite independent agencies to support needy musicians.

Romanticism

In rock, Romanticism still flourishes. All the Romantic archetypes of energy, passion, rebellion and demonism are still evident in the brawling, boozing bad boys of rock, storming from city to city on their lusty, groupie-dogged trail.

But the Romantic outlaw must have something to rebel against. The pioneers of rock were freaks, dreamers and malcontents who drew their lyricism and emotional power from the gritty rural traditions of white folk music and African-American blues.

Rock is a victim of its own success. What once signified rebellion is now only a high-school affectation. White suburban youth, rock's main audience, is trapped in creature comforts. Everything comes to them secondhand, through TV. And they no longer have direct contact with folk music and blues, the oral repository of centuries of love, hate, suffering and redemption.

In the Sixties, rock became the dominant musical form in America. And with the shift from singles to albums, which allowed for the marketing of personalities, it also became big business. The gilded formula froze into place. Today, scouts beat the bushes for young talent, squeeze a quick album out of the band, and put them on the road. "New" material is stressed. Albums featuring cover tunes of classics, as in the early Rolling Stones records, are discouraged.

From the moment the Beatles could not hear themselves sing

over the shrieking at Shea Stadium in the mid-Sixties, the rock concert format has become progressively less conducive to music-making. The enormous expense of huge sound systems and grandiose special effects has left no room for individualism and improvisation, no opportunity for the performers to respond to a particular audience or to their own moods. The show, with its army of technicians, is as fixed and rehearsed as the Ziegfeld Follies. Furthermore, the concert experience has degenerated. The focus has switched from the performance to raucous partying in the audience.

We Want to Rock

Music remains something that individual people experience in their own ways. Despite what they are fed by the mass media (the billboards, the record stores, counter people, radio stations), word of mouth—what band rocked, who you gotta see, and you gotta hear that tape—is still basically all about the power of music. And fear of the politically correct? We want to rock and have a good time, but we want to say something too. Some of our lyrics are a little pretentious or a little self-righteous, but I think that happens when you want to say something. We're trying to say what we think, trying to live what we feel. Everyone in our band is an American product, so we have a lot of prejudices. Anyone who is having a personal awakening and trying to say what you mean and affect a change may not always say what is politically correct. Political correctness is such a scam. Those people in academia who were really trying to move forward got slammed by political correctness. What was really going on in society, what people were really trying to say to each other, got dissed.

Communicator Peace of the rock group Power and Fear, *The Note*, May 1993.

These days, rock musicians are set upon by vulture managers, who sanitize and repackage them and strip them of their unruly free will. Like sports stars, musicians are milked to the max, then dropped and cast aside when their first album doesn't sell.

Managers offer all the temptations of Mammon to young rock bands: wealth, fame, and easy sex. There is not a single public voice in the culture to say to the musician: You are an artist, not a money machine. Don't sign the contract. Don't tour. Record only when you are ready. Go off on your own, like Jimi Hendrix, and live with your guitar until it becomes part of your body.

How should an artist be trained? Many English rock musicians in the Sixties and early Seventies, including John Lennon and Keith Richards, emerged from art schools. We must tell the young musician: Your peers are other artists, past and future.

Don't become a slave to the audience, with its smug hedonism, short attention span and hunger for hits.

Artists should immerse themselves in art. Two decades ago, rock musicians read poetry, studied Hinduism, and drew psychedelic visions in watercolors. For rock to move forward as an art form, our musicians must be given the opportunity for spiritual development. They should be encouraged to read, to look at paintings and foreign films, to listen to jazz and classical music.

Artists with a strong sense of vocation can survive life's disasters and triumphs with their inner lives intact. Our musicians need to be rescued from the carpetbaggers and gold-diggers who attack them when they are young and naïve. Long, productive careers don't happen by chance.

"[Madonna's] artistic imagination ripples and eddies with the inner currents in American music."

Madonna Has Liberated American Women

Camille Paglia

Continuing to pursue her longtime interest in the art and culture of sensual excess, Camille Paglia here explores Madonna's artistic technique and use of historical symbolism. For instance, Paglia describes Madonna as a "Venus stepping from the radio waves"— consciously almost a mythological figure. Furthermore, Paglia claims that Madonna's Catholic youth formed the basis for her sensuality and the constant tension in it between repression and sexual freedom. For Paglia, Madonna has come to embody "the restless individualism of Western personality."

As you read, consider the following questions:

1. What does Paglia mean when she says Madonna uses disco music "liturgically"? How is religion important to Madonna?
2. How does the author contrast Madonna and Marilyn Monroe?
3. Why, according to Paglia, do "old-guard establishment feminists" still loathe Madonna?

Camille Paglia, "Madonna II: Venus of the Radio Waves," *The Independent on Sunday Review*, July 21, 1991. Reprinted by permission.

I'm a dyed-in-the-wool, true-blue Madonna fan.

It all started in 1984, when Madonna exploded onto MTV with a brazen, insolent, in-your-face American street style, which she had taken from urban blacks, Hispanics, and her own middle-class but turbulent and charismatic Italian-American family. From the start, there was a flamboyant and parodistic element to her sexuality, a hard glamour she had learned from Hollywood cinema and from its devotees, gay men and drag queens.

Madonna is a dancer. She thinks and expresses herself through dance, which exists in the eternal Dionysian realm of music. Dance, which she studied with a gay man in her home state of Michigan, was her avenue of escape from the conventions of religion and bourgeois society. The sensual language of her body allowed her to transcend the over-verbalized codes of her class and time.

Madonna's great instinctive intelligence was evident to me from her earliest videos. My first fights about her had to do with whether she was a good dancer or merely a well-coached one. As year by year she built up the remarkable body of her video work, with its dazzling number of dance styles, I have had to fight about that less and less. However, I am still at war about her with feminists and religious conservatives (an illuminating alliance of contemporary puritans).

Most people who denigrate Madonna do so out of ignorance. The postwar baby-boom generation in America, to which I belong, has been deeply immersed in popular culture for thirty-five years. Our minds were formed by rock music, which has poured for twenty-four hours a day from hundreds of noisy, competitive independent radio stations around the country.

Madonna, like Venus stepping from the radio waves, emerged from this giant river of music. Her artistic imagination ripples and eddies with the inner currents in American music. She is at her best when she follows her intuition and speaks to the world in the universal language of music and dance. She is at her worst when she tries to define and defend herself in words, which she borrows from louche, cynical pals and shallow, single-issue political activists.

A Command of Disco

Madonna consolidates and fuses several traditions of pop music, but the major one she typifies is disco, which emerged in the Seventies and, under the bland commercial rubric "dance music," is still going strong. It has a terrible reputation: when you say the word *disco*, people think "Bee Gees." But I view disco, at its serious best, as a dark, grand Dionysian music with roots in African earth-cult.

Madonna's command of massive, resonant bass lines, which she heard in the funky dance clubs of Detroit and New York, has always impressed me. As an Italian Catholic, she uses them liturgically. Like me, she sensed the buried pagan religiosity in disco. I recall my stunned admiration as I sat in the theater in 1987 and first experienced the crashing, descending chords of Madonna's "Causing a Commotion," which opened her dreadful movie, *Who's That Girl?* If you want to hear the essence of modernity, listen to those chords, infernal, apocalyptic, and grossly sensual. This is the authentic voice of the *fin de siècle*.

© Dan Lynch. Reprinted with permission.

Madonna's first video, for her superb, drivingly lascivious disco hit "Burnin' Up," did not make much of an impression. The platinum-blonde girl kneeling and emoting in the middle of a midnight highway just seemed to be a band member's floozie. In retrospect, the video, with its rapid, cryptic surrealism, prefigures Madonna's signature themes and contains moments of eerie erotic poetry.

"Lucky Star" was Madonna's breakthrough video. Against a luminous, white abstract background, she and two impassive dancers perform a synchronized series of jagged, modern kicks and steps. Wearing the ragtag outfit of all-black bows, see-through netting, fingerless lace gloves, bangle bracelets, dangle earrings, chains, crucifixes, and punk booties that would set off a gigantic fashion craze among American adolescent girls, Madonna flaunts her belly button and vamps the camera with a smoky, piercing, come-hither-but-keep-your-distance stare. Here she first suggests her striking talent for improvisational floor work, which she would spectacularly demonstrate at the first MTV awards show, when, wrapped in a white-lace wedding dress, she campily rolled and undulated snakelike on the stage, to the baffled consternation of the first rows of spectators.

Lucky Star

I remember sitting in a bar when "Lucky Star," just out, appeared on TV. The stranger perched next to me, a heavyset, middle-aged working-class woman, watched the writhing Madonna and, wide-eyed and slightly frowning, blankly said, her beer held motionless halfway to her lips, "Will you look at this." There was a sense that Madonna was doing something so new and so strange that one didn't know whether to call it beautiful or grotesque. Through MTV, Madonna was transmitting an avant-garde downtown New York sensibility to the American masses.

In "Lucky Star," Madonna is raffish, gamine, still full of the street-urchin mischief that she would portray in her first and best film, Susan Seidelman's *Desperately Seeking Susan* (1984). In "Borderline," she shows her burgeoning star quality. As the girlfriend of Hispanic toughs who is picked up by a British photographer and makes her first magazine cover, she presents the new dualities of her life: the gritty, multiracial street and club scene that she had haunted in obscurity and poverty, and her new slick, fast world of popularity and success.

In one shot of "Borderline," as she chummily chews gum with kidding girlfriends on the corner, you can see the nondescript plainness of Madonna's real face, which she again exposes, with admirable candor, in *Truth or Dare* when, slurping soup and sporting a shower cap over hair rollers, she fences with her conservative Italian father over the phone. Posing for the photographer in "Borderline," Madonna in full cry fixes the camera lens with challenging, molten eyes, in a bold ritual display of sex and aggression. This early video impressed me with Madonna's sophisticated view of the fabrications of femininity, that exquisite theater which feminism condemns as oppression but which I see as a supreme artifact of civilization. I sensed then, and now know for certain, that Madonna, like me, is drawn to drag queens for their daring, flamboyant insight into sex roles, which they see far more clearly and historically than do our endlessly

131

complaining feminists.

Madonna's first major video, in artistic terms, was "Like a Virgin," where she began to release her flood of inner sexual personae, which appear and disappear like the painted creatures of masque. Madonna is an orchid-heavy Veronese duchess in white, a febrile Fassbinder courtesan in black, a slutty nun-turned-harlequin flapping a gold cross and posturing, bum in air, like a demonic phantom in the nose of a gondola. This video alone, with its coruscating polarities of evil and innocence, would be enough to establish Madonna's artistic distinction for the next century.

In "Material Girl," where she sashays around in Marilyn Monroe's strapless red gown and archly flashes her fan at a pack of men in tuxedos, Madonna first showed her flair for comedy. Despite popular opinion, there are no important parallels between Madonna and Monroe, who was a virtuoso comedienne but who was insecure, depressive, passive-aggressive, and infuriatingly obstructionist in her career habits. Madonna is manic, perfectionist, workaholic. Monroe abused alcohol and drugs, while Madonna shuns them. Monroe had a tentative, melting, dreamy solipsism; Madonna has Judy Holliday's wisecracking smart mouth and Joan Crawford's steel will and bossy, circus-master managerial competence.

In 1985 the cultural resistance to Madonna became overt. Despite the fact that her "Into the Groove," the mesmerizing theme song of *Desperately Seeking Susan*, had saturated our lives for nearly a year, the Grammy Awards outrageously ignored her. The feminist and moralist sniping began in earnest. Madonna "degraded" womanhood; she was vulgar, sacrilegious, stupid, shallow, opportunistic. A nasty mass quarrel broke out in one of my classes between the dancers, who adored Madonna, and the actresses, who scorned her.

Open Your Heart

I knew the quality of what I was seeing: "Open Your Heart," with its risqué peep-show format, remains for me not only Madonna's greatest video but one of the three or four best videos ever made. In the black bustier she made famous (transforming the American lingerie industry overnight), Madonna, bathed in blue-white light, plays Marlene Dietrich straddling a chair. Her eyes are cold, distant, all-seeing. She is ringed, as if in a sea-green aquarium, by windows of lewd or longing voyeurs: sad sacks, brooding misfits, rowdy studs, dreamy gay twins, a melancholy lesbian.

"Open Your Heart" is a brilliant mimed psychodrama of the interconnections between art and pornography, love and lust. Madonna won my undying loyalty by reviving and re-creating the hard glamour of the studio-era Hollywood movie queens, figures of mythological grandeur. Contemporary feminism cut itself off from history and bankrupted itself when it spun its puerile, paranoid fantasy of male oppressors and female sex-object victims. Woman is the dominant sex. Woman's sexual glamour has bewitched and destroyed men since Delilah and Helen of Troy. Madonna, role model to millions of girls world-wide, has cured the ills of feminism by reasserting woman's command of the sexual realm.

Responding to the spiritual tensions within Italian Catholicism, Madonna discovered the buried paganism within the church. The torture of Christ and the martyrdom of the saints, represented in lurid polychrome images, dramatize the passions of the body, repressed in art-fearing puritan Protestantism of the kind that still lingers in America. Playing with the outlaw personae of prostitute and dominatrix, Madonna has made a major contribution to the history of women. She has rejoined and healed the split halves of woman: Mary, the Blessed Virgin and holy mother, and Mary Magdalene, the harlot.

The Expression of the Whore's Power

The old-guard establishment feminists who still loathe Madonna have a sexual ideology problem. I am radically pro-pornography and pro-prostitution. Hence I perceive Madonna's strutting sexual exhibitionism not as cheapness or triviality but as the full, florid expression of the whore's ancient rule over men. Incompetent amateurs have given prostitution a bad name. In my university office in Philadelphia hangs a pagan shrine: a life-size full-color cardboard display of Joanne Whalley-Kilmer and Bridget Fonda naughtily smiling in scanty, skintight gowns as Christine Keeler and Mandy Rice-Davies in the film *Scandal*. I tell visitors it is "my political science exhibit." For me, the Profumo affair symbolizes the evanescence of male government compared to woman's cosmic power.

In a number of videos, Madonna has played with bisexual innuendos, reaching their culmination in the solemn woman-to-woman kiss of "Justify My Love," a deliciously decadent sarabande of transvestite and sadomasochistic personae that was banned by MTV. Madonna is again pioneering here, this time in restoring lesbian eroticism to the continuum of heterosexual response, from which it was unfortunately removed twenty years ago by lesbian feminist separatists of the most boring, humorless, strident kind. "Justify My Love" springs from the sophisticated European art films of the Fifties and Sixties that shaped my sexual imagination in college. It shows bisexuality and all experimentation as a liberation from false, narrow categories.

Madonna's inner emotional life can be heard in the smooth,

transparent "La Isla Bonita," one of her most perfect songs, with its haunting memory of paradise lost. No one ever mentions it. Publicity has tended to focus instead on the more blatantly message-heavy videos, like "Papa Don't Preach," with its teen pregnancy, or "Express Yourself," where feminist cheerleading lyrics hammer on over crisp, glossy images of bedroom bondage, dungeon torture, and epicene, crotch-grabbing Weimar elegance.

"Like a Prayer" gave Pepsi-Cola dyspepsia: Madonna receives the stigmata, makes love with the animated statue of a black saint, and dances in a rumpled silk slip in front of a field of burning crosses. This last item, with its uncontrolled racial allusions, shocked even me. But Madonna has a strange ability to remake symbolism in her own image. Kitsch and trash are transformed by her high-energy dancer's touch, her earnest yet over-the-top drag-queen satire.

A Crusader Against Repression

Madonna wants (by her own admission) to "press buttons" and provoke us to rethink socially accepted understandings of female behavior. Mixing masculine and feminine gender roles, she is able to react against a sexually repressive society that "educates" women into rigid gender roles which inhibit their freedom and foster passivity in social relations, including sex.

Kathleen Talvacchia, *Christianity and Crisis*, July 15, 1991.

The "Vogue" video approaches "Open Your Heart" in quality. Modelling her glowing, languorous postures on the great high-glamour photographs of Hurrell, Madonna reprises the epiphanic iconography of our modern Age of Hollywood. Feminism is infested with white, middle-class, literary twits ignorant of art and smugly hostile to fashion photography and advertisement, which contain the whole history of art. In the dramatic chiaroscuro compositions of "Vogue," black and Hispanic New York drag queens, directly inspired by fashion magazines, display the arrogant aristocracy of beauty, recognized as divine by Plato and, before him, by the princes of Egypt.

In my own theoretical terms, Madonna has both the dynamic Dionysian power of dance and the static Apollonian power of iconicism. Part of her fantastic success has been her ability to communicate with the still camera, a talent quite separate from any other. To project to a camera, you must have an autoerotic autonomy, a sharp self-conceptualization, even a fetishistic perversity: the camera is a machine you make love to. Madonna has been fortunate in finding Herb Ritts, who has recorded the dazzling profusion of her mercurial sexual personae. Through still photography, she has blanketed the world press with her image between videos and concert tours. But Madonna, I contend, never does anything just for publicity. Rather, publicity is the language naturally used by the great stars to communicate with their vast modern audience. Through publicity, we live in the star's flowing consciousness.

Madonna has evolved physically. In a charming early live video, "Dress You Up," she is warm, plump, and flirty under pink and powder-blue light. Her voice is enthusiastic but thin and breathy. She began to train both voice and body, so that her present silhouette, with some erotic loss, is wiry and muscular, hyperkinetic for acrobatic dance routines based on the martial arts. Madonna is notorious for monthly or even weekly changes of hair color and style, by which she embodies the restless individualism of Western personality. Children love her. As with the Beatles, this is always the sign of a monumental pop phenomenon.

A Complex Modern Woman

Madonna has her weak moments: for example, I have no tolerance for the giggling baby talk that she periodically hauls out of the closet, as over the final credits of *Truth or Dare*. She is a complex modern woman. Indeed, that is the main theme of her extraordinary achievement. She is exploring the problems and tensions of being an ambitious woman today. Like the potent Barbra Streisand, whose maverick female style had a great impact on American girls in the Sixties, Madonna is confronting the romantic dilemma of the strong woman looking for a man but uncertain whether she wants a tyrant or slave. The tigress in heat is drawn to surrender but may kill her conqueror.

In "Open Your Heart," Madonna is woman superbly alone, master of her own fate. Offstage at the end, she mutates into an androgynous boy-self and runs off. "What a Tramp!," thundered the *New York Post* in a recent full-page headline. Yes, Madonna has restored the Whore of Babylon, the pagan goddess banned by the last book of the Bible. With an instinct for world-domination gained from Italian Catholicism, she has rolled like a juggernaut over the multitude of her carping critics. This is a kaleidoscopic career still in progress. But Madonna's most enduring cultural contribution may be that she has introduced ravishing visual beauty and a lush Mediterranean sensuality into parched, pinched, word-drunk Anglo-Saxon feminism.

> *"Never has the structure of incentives been so favorable to artistic martyrdom."*

Madonna Is a Vapid Pop Figure

Joseph Sobran

In the following viewpoint, Joseph Sobran examines the media image of Madonna, and argues that she has carefully calculated and constructed it for lucrative shock value. He further contends that Madonna lacks consistency, honesty, and character, content to excite audiences with lurid performances of no artistic merit or intellectual content. Sobran particularly objects to Madonna's use of religious imagery in sexual displays. For some years, Sobran has been a syndicated newspaper columnist, and is presently critic-at-large for the conservative journal *National Review*.

As you read, consider the following questions:

1. One of Sobran's main charges against Madonna is that she is a calculating artist, rather than a principled one. What evidence does he give to support this charge?
2. What has been the role of the imagery of the Catholic church in Madonna's performances? What is her view of the church?
3. Sobran contends that Madonna is obsessed with her Self. What examples of this obsession does he cite? Why is such an obsession meaningful to her audiences?

Joseph Sobran, "Single Sex and the Girl," *National Review*, August 12, 1991, © 1991 by National Review, Inc., 150 E. 35th St., New York, NY 10016. Reprinted with permission.

In one scene in *Truth or Dare*—a documentary, of sorts, of her "Blond Ambition" concert tour—Madonna phones her father to ask if he's coming to see her perform. He says he understands her act is pretty "racy" and inquires as to whether she'll "tone it down" for him and the family. No, she answers; she won't "compromise my artistic integrity."

A few minutes later, we see that uncompromised artistic integrity as she lies on a bed onstage. The stage is dark, except for the bed. Standing beside her are two black male dancers wearing weird conical brassieres. As she sings "Like a Virgin," she vigorously massages her crotch, moaning and arching her back spasmodically. There's more, but you get the basic idea. The huge crowd goes wild.

Madonna is a genius at getting attention. Everything she does gets attention—her records, her videos, her movies, her marriage, her divorce, her amours (including a joke that she'd had a lesbian relationship with the comedienne Sandra Bernhard). When she showed up at the Cannes Film Festival with her hair dyed a new color, her face appeared on the front page of the New York *Daily News*. She has been on the cover of every magazine except *National Geographic*.

How does she do it? As she admits, she's not a great singer, a great dancer, or even—at least in repose—a great looker. She can't act. Yet she has the most flamboyantly theatrical personality since . . . well, who was the last one? Bette Davis? Joan Crawford? Tallulah Bankhead? Some people have what I can only call contagious vanity. You may even dislike them, but you can't take your eyes off them. Madonna is like that. In a country where people want to be liked (maybe even more ardently than they want to be loved), she dares you to hate her.

"Madonna is the true feminist," writes Camille Paglia, herself a sort of antifeminist feminist. "She exposes the puritanism and suffocating ideology of American feminism . . . Madonna has taught young women to be fully female and sexual while still exercising total control over their lives. She shows girls how to be attractive, sensual, energetic, ambitious, aggressive, and funny—all at the same time."

Kink and Danger

She's undeniably magnetic, but it's a calculating magnetism, a carefully constructed aura of kink and danger. If she seems to be shattering conventions, she's also there to pick up the pieces. One of her steamier videos, "Like a Prayer," shows her in a Catholic church adoring a statue of a black saint, who comes to life and kisses her passionately. She receives the stigmata, and there are burning crosses and things, and . . . well, again, you get the idea: a deliberate fusion of such themes as sex, race, and

137

religion. These elements are combined in surreal montage, and the effect is eerie, shocking, Weimar decadent.

An even more explicit video, "Justify My Love," did succeed in outraging people, and even easygoing MTV refused to play it. "The video is pornographic," Miss Paglia writes. "It's decadent. And it's fabulous. MTV was right to ban it." But she chides Madonna for copping out on *Nightline* by pleading "her love of children, her social activism, and her condom endorsements." If you want to shock people, go ahead and shock 'em. But don't blame them for *being* shocked.

A Limited Perspective

Madonna is a bad actress, a barely adequate singer, a graceless dancer, a boring interview subject, a workmanlike but uninspired (co)songwriter, and a dynamo of hard work and ferocious ambition. . . . Her pool of ideas, derived from a diligent study of iconology, is limited.

Luc Sante, *The New Republic*, August 20, 1990.

The trouble is that Madonna wants to have it both ways. (One problem in writing about her is that everything tends to sound like a double-entendre.) She clearly knows what she's doing, but wants to pretend she doesn't. Her calculation is shown in one sequence in *Truth or Dare* when her tour arrives in Toronto and she is told that the police are prepared to arrest her if she does the masturbation bit. She asks what the penalty is. She learns she'll probably just be booked, fined, and released. This, to her, is a cheap price to pay for the international front-page publicity she stands to get, so she goes ahead with it. The cops back down and do nothing. Never has the structure of incentives been so favorable to artistic martyrdom.

A similar event occurs in Italy, where she finds on her arrival that the Vatican has denounced her in advance. She holds a press conference and says that as an Italian-American she resents this prejudicial treatment. Hers is no "conventional" rock act, but "a total theatrical experience." The note of pique sounds sincere enough, but she also knows that in her terms the Vatican has done her a favor. Madonna has a keen sense of whom it's profitable to offend and whom it isn't. She surrounds herself with blacks and homosexuals. She is heavy into AIDS education: "Next to Hitler, AIDS is the worst thing to happen in the twentieth century," she told *Vanity Fair* recently—a good, conventional, and convenient view to hold in her line of work. And when the Simon Wiesenthal Center in Los Angeles attacked her for including the phrase "synagogue of Satan" (from the Book of Revelation) in one of her songs, she apologized.

In the film, one of her dancers worries that his scene of simulated sex with her will hurt his career. "In this country it works the other way around," she answers. "The more notorious you are, the more you are going to work! Don't you guys understand that?" Indeed. Nothing is more conventional than the daring. In *Truth or Dare*, she talks nonstop raunch, bares her breasts, gets into bed with a naked dancer and whoops about the size of his organ (it's all right, he's gay), and much, much more.

The Good Christian

Raised a Catholic by devout parents (her mother died when she was six), Madonna's target of choice is Catholicism. Her concert and video performances abound in crucifixes, dancers dressed as priests fondling her, and so forth. It's exciting. It's outrageous. It sells. Naturally, much of her following consists of lapsed Catholics, typified by the columnist Pete Hamill, who calls her "a good Christian." You can write a Hamill column with your eyes closed: Jesus preferred Mary Magdalene to the Pharisees, drove the money-changers out of the Temple, hated prigs—a lot like Pete Hamill, come to think of it. This sort of approval (terribly smug, in its own way) implies that because Jesus forgave unchastity, he didn't regard it as a sin. Not only is this a non sequitur, it overlooks some very stern words in the Gospels, sterner, in fact, than anything in Saint Paul, the favorite scapegoat of lapsed Christians who want to insist that it's only the *Church* they object to—nothing against Jesus, you understand.

Charity is of course the supreme Christian virtue, and those who fail in chastity often insist that they make up for it in charity. But there is more than one way of being uncharitable, and self-serving solicitude for today's accredited victims—"compassion," for short—doesn't necessarily cover a multitude of sins. In *Truth or Dare* we learn that Madonna leads her troupe in prayer before every performance. But the tone of her prayer is imperious and stagy. The viewer wonders if praying with the boss—or rather standing there submissively while *she* prays—is part of the job description of dancer. The question acquires a special urgency when the prayer turns into a chewing-out of some of those in the circle. She stops just short of demanding divine retribution against those who have offended her.

Madonna is even less charitable toward the Church itself. "I've always known that Catholicism is a completely sexist, repressed, sin- and punishment-based religion," she told an interviewer for *Us* magazine. She was even blunter to *Vanity Fair*: "I think it's disgusting. I think it's hypocritical. And it's unloving.

It's not what God and Christianity are all about." Nearly every interview she gives includes bitter remarks about the Church and its "rules." It's the only subject, apart from herself, she regularly talks about.

But her father is still a faithful Catholic, and in *Truth or Dare* we see her fretting at the idea of his seeing her perform "Like a Virgin." In fact she *does* "tone it down" when he's in the audience, and she hales him onto the stage to be introduced to the crowd. He seems a mild fellow, confusedly proud of his famous daughter. Her anxiety about being seen by him *in flagrante* is puzzling: she seems bent on offending everyone who believes in the things he believes in, but not *him*. Why this exemption? If she hates the faith she was raised in, why doesn't she blame the man who raised her?

"She doesn't want to live off-camera," jokes Warren Beatty, her beau at the time of the filming. "Why would you bother to say something if it's off-camera?" Because Madonna finds everything about Madonna absolutely fascinating, that's why. Imagine a film in which it's left to Warren Beatty to sound the note of common sense.

"I find myself drawn to emotional cripples," Madonna says, explaining the odd assortment of characters she surrounds herself with. "I like to play mother." Oh. We see her visiting her own mother's grave (for the first time); naturally, she dresses in black for the occasion, brings a camera crew along, and lies down to kiss the tombstone. We see her backstage, complaining about a mike failure to a hapless technician. We see her dining with friends. We see her shopping in Paris. We see her meeting an old school chum, who she tells us once did something naughty to her at a pajama party. (The school chum, now a mother of five, denies it when informed of it; she looks shocked by this ambush, having named a daughter Madonna.) We see her telling someone or another that her mission is to be "provocative" and "political." We see, in fact, two hours of this carefully staged "spontaneity," and two hours trapped in a dark room with *that* ego feels like a week.

The Real Madonna

Talking to *Vanity Fair*, Madonna gets defensive: "People will say, 'She knows the camera is on, she's just acting.' But even if I *am* acting, there's a truth in my acting . . . You could watch it and say, I still don't know Madonna, and *good*. Because you will never know the real me. Ever." You mean there's *more*?

Well, if we never know the real Madonna, we won't have Madonna to blame for it. She talks about herself volubly, incessantly; she poses for photo stills dressed up as Marilyn Monroe and other sexpots. It's as if her privacy might unfairly deprive us of something. Or rather, as if she wanted to *become* all the fascinating women of the past, and reveal their mysteries to us. Instead she creates the disconcerting impression that all the mystery may have been bogus; maybe those women *were* like her: self-absorbed little bores who talked in clichés about "art" and "truth," when they weren't talking about themselves. One would rather not know.

As for "truth," Madonna isn't interested in any that may inconvenience her. It never crosses her mind that there may be more to Catholicism than her spiteful parody of it, which is of an order of glibness that would embarrass Phil Donahue. For her there is no fundamental order in life, only arbitrary "rules." Do whatcha want, as long as you practice "safe sex," that mirage of those who think selfishness and sensuality can be calculating and civic-minded even at the peak of ardor. It isn't just that she's hopelessly banal whenever she tries to share an insight. It's that she has reached that pitch of egomania at which celebrity supposes itself oracular. That's when you say things like "Power is a great aphrodisiac," and you think it sounds impressive. (We may note in passing that the Me Decade is now entering its third decade.)

Junior High All Over Again

In many ways, Madonna sounds like junior high all over again—the same confusion and anger, the insensitivity on everybody's part, the same inability to reckon with the consequences of appearance and image. In many ways, she is the stellar product of the environment that produced her—which means contemporary pop culture itself, with all its male domination, juvenalia, and lust to consume before being consumed.

Dave Marsh, *The First Rock and Roll Confidential Report*, 1985.

And as for "art," well, philosophers differ. But it's widely believed by wise people that art and ego sit uneasily together. The true artist, even if his ego is as muscular as Beethoven's, creates something outside himself. Art is not "self-expression" in the sense that its focus of interest lies in its creator; rather, it is self-contained. Its value doesn't depend on our knowledge of the artist. *Hamlet* is a great play no matter who wrote it. *Parsifal* is a great opera even if Wagner did compose it.

But for Madonna, art is defined by the censors: it's whatever they don't like. So someone who gets the censors howling must be an artist.

Silly, but a lot of people agree with her, and they buy tickets.

Madonna offers something new under the sun: vicarious self-absorption. It takes a special kind of imagination to identify with a solipsist.

Madonna just doesn't glory in herself: she glories in her *self*. And *Truth or Dare* suggests a novel ambition: to make the self, even in its private moments, an object of universal attention. Who was the love of your life? someone asks her. "Sean," she murmurs, meaning her ex-husband, Sean Penn (of whom it was once said that he had slugged every photographer except Karsh of Ottawa). Sean, she explains, was madly jealous and domineering, but "at least he paid attention." Better hostile attention than none at all.

Like most pop music, Madonna's songs are about love. But love is the subject about which she shows no understanding at all. She is the perfect expression of an age that has reduced the erotic to the sensual: the gratification of the self rather than the yearning for union with another. "Lovers" become interchangeable and succeed each other quickly, each being merely instrumental to the self and its cravings. Real love is like art: it demands the subordination of the ego. Kinky, exciting, shocking: these are the attributes of love as she conceives it. It would make no sense to tell her that sodomy is at best a stunted and misdirected form of eros, since heterosexual love, as she exemplifies it, has the same character. The purpose of this love is neither permanent union nor procreation, but pleasure and ego-enhancement. For her, in fact, the erotic isn't all that different from the autoerotic, except that there happens to be another person present.

But the word *autoerotic* is self-contradictory. Being in love with yourself isn't love. And having sex with yourself hardly qualifies as sex. The Victorians thought masturbation led to blindness. If they'd said moral blindness, they might have had a point. At least Madonna seems to intimate a connection. "Masturbation," Woody Allen has said, "is having sex with someone you love." When we watch Madonna doing "Like a Virgin," clutching her private parts (if they can be called private anymore), simulating ecstatic convulsions, we're seeing her having sex, as it were, with someone she loves, all right—maybe the only one she *can* love.

> *"[Rap] is a cultural black hole able to suck up r&b, rock, go-go, house and, soon, Third World rhythms without losing its combative personality."*

Rap Music Is Liberating

Nelson George

Throughout the 1980s, Nelson George's essays regularly appeared in the New York weekly newspaper *The Village Voice*. Described by Cornel West as "the leading critic of African-American popular culture of his generation," George is the author of several books and collections of cultural commentary. In the following viewpoint, George argues that black culture has maintained its vitality and drive, continually emerging from a painful yet hopeful urban underground reality.

As you read, consider the following questions:

1. What was the nature of the audience when rap first emerged? How has rap evolved or developed as a social phenomenon?
2. George says rap "isn't a music; it's a cultural black hole." What does he mean by that? What has rap "crystallized"?
3. How in George's view is rap threatened by commercialization?

Excerpts from *Buppies, B-Boys, Baps, and Bohos: Notes on Post-Soul Black Culture* by Nelson George, © 1992 by Nelson George. Reprinted by permission of HarperCollins Publishers, Inc.

Ten years ago the Sugar Hill Gang's "Rapper's Delight" was on the radio, and, in Brooklyn's Birdel's on Nostrand Avenue, owner Joe Long was selling boxloads of 12-inches. The single was hitting so hard and fast that Sugarhill Records hadn't even made logos yet; they slapped on orange stickers with so little information it made them look like bootlegs. I remember Joe smiling and saying that "Rapper's Delight" was "the hottest thing in the street in a long time."

Ten years ago in SoHo's earth-toned Greene Street studio, accustomed to hosting John Cage and Phillip Glass, two *Billboard* magazine employees, Robert Ford, Jr., and J.B. Moore, were recording a record called "Christmas Rappin'" with a Harlem homie, Curtis Walker, a/k/a Kurtis Blow. Bassist Larry Smith (later to produce Whodini and Run-D.M.C.), Joey "Son-of-Kurtis Blow" Simmons (later Run of Run-D.M.C.), and Blow's manager Russell "Rush" Simmons (later rap's biggest manager) were among the many then-obscure folks who stopped by to joke, laugh, and ponder the recording process. Rap records? Well, it had worked for those no-talent Sugar Gangers. Still, we wondered if anyone would buy more than one rap record.

Ten years ago, at a schoolyard in the South Bronx, Cool Here rolled up in a van with turntables and records. A crowd of kids waited. After plugging his equipment into the base of a streetlight, Here scratched beats from "Bongo Rock" and *Shaft in Africa* and other obscure records until well after dusk. Surprisingly few people danced. Most of the overwhelmingly male crowd hovered around the turntables, peeking over each other on tiptoes and trying to figure out which records contained which beat.

Ten years later I can see rap's triumph not simply as musical but as social. It crystallized a post-civil rights, ultra-urban, unromantic, hyperrealistic, neonationalistic, antiassimilationist, aggressive Afrocentric impulse reflecting the thoughts of city kids more deeply than the celebrated crossover icons Michael Jackson-Bill Cosby-Oprah Winfrey et al. This was music funneled through Bruce Lee, Mr. Magic, Bootsy and George "Dr. Funkenstein" Clinton, *Scarface*, Sylvia Robinson, Magic versus Bird, Jesse Jackson, Ed Koch, James Brown, *A Clockwork Orange*, Malcolm X, Pee-wee Herman, Nelson Mandela, Frankie Crocker, Michael Jordan, "Miami Vice," and the Smurfs. It emerged cartoony, antimelodic, brooding, materialistic, entrepreneurial, chauvinistic, user-friendly, genital conscious, and always spoiling for a fight.

A New World View

Hip hop became the catchall for the culture of clothes, slang, dances, and philosophies that sprang up in the '80s. But rap on records—words as rhythm, weapon, metaphor—represented a new worldview just as soul music did in the '60s and disco, sadly, did in the '70s. Rap, however, isn't a music. It's a cultural black hole able to suck up r&b, rock, go-go, house and, soon, Third World rhythms without losing its combative personality. Every time I've thought its energy was flagging, new beats ("Planet Rock," "Sucker M.C.s," "Eric B. Is President," "Bring the Noise," "It Takes Two," "Me, Myself & I") made things hectic all over again.

For me rap was a professional and aesthetic inspiration. The first two pieces I sold to this paper were on DJ Lovebug Starski and Grandmaster Flash & the Furious Five, and it was rap that got me bylines at several other publications. Rap's ability to be righteously, uncompromisingly black yet speak to mixed audiences proved to me the power of undiluted African American thought, both as a celebration of our people and a critique of the whitebread mainstream.

A History of Rap

Rap's forbears stretch back through disco, street funk, radio DJs, Bo Diddley, the bebop singers, Cab Calloway, Pigmeat Markham, the tap dancers, and comics. The Last Poets, Gil Scott-Heron, Muhammad Ali, a cappella and doo-wop groups, ring games, skip-rope rhymes, prison and army songs, toast, signifying and the dozens, all the way to the *griots* of Nigeria and Gambia. No matter how far it penetrates into the twilight maze of Japanese video games and cool European electronics, its roots are still the deepest in all contemporary Afro-American music.

David Troop, *Rap Attack*, 1984.

The question is no longer, "Will rap last?" but "Who will control it?" The major labels' racial and class prejudices kept them out of rap well past the time its commercial viability had been proven. Now MCA and Atlantic, following the lead of CBS and Warner Bros., are signing every halfway decent act they can. The number one record on *Billboard*'s black album chart is by D.O.C., a Los Angeles-based rapper on Atlantic. That he's number one is no surprise—he's part of the super-hot N.W.A-Eazy E posse—but that he's from Dallas and on Atlantic, considering this genre's East Coast and indie record company roots, is a sign of the new times.

It is also potentially quite troubling. One of the elements that diluted r&b in the last generation has been the majors' noisome meddling. Too many records issued—too many bad records issued—too little personalized artist development, too many folks promoting and marketing it with zip understanding of its audience or traditions, led r&b into a creative impasse that, lately, only hip hop-influenced producers have unblocked.

Equally wack, black radio has yet to fully understand this movement. Rap shows are slotted in fringe time, rarely receiving primetime airplay corresponding to its sales. Because of this I-don't-want-to-know attitude, black radio will confuse bad rap with good, because it hasn't developed the aesthetic judgment to tell them apart. These quality-blind priorities are especially dangerous when major labels push lame acts like the Fat Boys and J.J. Fad.

To proclaim the death of rap is, to be sure, premature. But the farther the control of rap gets from its street-corner constituency and the more corporations grasp it—record conglomerates, Burger King and Minute Maid, "Yo! MTV Raps," etc.—the more vulnerable it becomes to cultural emasculation.

> "The content of rap can be summarized in terms of two criticisms, that it is obscene and that it is 'sexist.'"

Rap Music Is Decadent

Terry Teachout

Combining a longtime interest in classic jazz and conservative politics, Terry Teachout explores the background and context of rap music in the following viewpoint. While acknowledging that some rap extols self-help and the teaching of black history in the public schools, Teachout believes that rap is seriously flawed by its own brand of racial stereotyping and prejudicial language.

As you read, consider the following questions:

1. How, according to Teachout, does rap portray women? White people? Jews?
2. What role does Teachout say "Black Muslim demonology" has played in the music of Public Enemy? Is this to be found in all rap music?
3. Why is the theme of genocidal violence so prevalent in rap? Who do rappers believe is responsible for violence in our society?

From Terry Teachout, "Rap and Racism." Reprinted from *Commentary*, March 1990, with permission; all rights reserved.

For the average middle-class listener, whether black or white, rap music is a landscape too alien for anything but discomfort. That rap is loud, aggressive, and often obscene is the least of it. Every New Yorker who reads the papers knows that the teenagers who allegedly raped and brutalized a woman jogger in Central Park entertained themselves after their arrest by collectively chanting the lyrics to "Wild Thing," a popular record by the Los Angeles rapper Tone-Loc. Many well-informed Americans know, too, that a member of the rap group Public Enemy gave an interview to the Washington *Times* in which he delivered an anti-Semitic tirade of shocking virulence. And yet rap now fills the most popular daily program on MTV. It has been called by the composer Quincy Jones "the jazz of the 90's." And it has been described by Jon Pareles of the New York *Times* as "the most startlingly original and fastest-growing genre in popular music.". . .

Rap

In most raps, the rapper "disses" (attacks) other rappers and asserts his own superior verbal skills. Many raps consist solely of this kind of boasting. Beyond that, the content of rap can be summarized in terms of two commonly leveled criticisms, that it is obscene and that it is "sexist." Indeed, most rappers do make elaborate use of profanity, and also equate verbal with sexual prowess. Rapping is itself an outgrowth of "the dozens," a highly competitive verbal game of rhyming sexual insults developed between the world wars in the ghettos of urban America. Just as victory in this game is understood as a token of sexual superiority, so the verbally proficient rapper is assumed to be sexually proficient in like degree. When L.L. Cool J (short for "Ladies Love Cool James") proclaims "No rapper can rap quite like I can/I'll take a muscle-bound man and put his face in the sand," the implication is clear.

Not surprisingly, women in the world of rap are largely, if not exclusively, objects of transient sexual gratification. Many raps consist of a graphic description of a night's trolling. ("Evil 'E' was out coolin' with a freak one night/Fucked the bitch with a flashlight/Pulled it out and left he batteries in/So he could get a charge when he begin.") In the world of rap it is the destiny of women to be picked up, casually fornicated with, and left behind by their men. . . .

Some rappers, to be sure, are quite far removed from the life evoked by lyrics like these. Run-D.M.C., for instance, is an extremely popular ensemble of thoroughly middle-class black teens who have endorsed Adidas sneakers and Coca-Cola; DJ Jazzy Jeff and the Fresh Prince, a clean-cut rap team that has successfully "crossed over" to a fully integrated mainstream teenage audi-

ence, specialize in sanitized raps like "Parents Just Don't Understand" ("She said, 'What's wrong? This shirt cost twenty dollars!'/I said, 'Mom! This shirt is plaid with a butterfly collar!'").
But such sentiments are comparatively rare. More typical is
Ice-T, a former member of a Los Angeles gang, whose raps are
mosaics of sex and violence in which the brutality of street life
in a culture where drugs are sold around the clock is taken for
granted. His 1988 album *Power* features on its jacket a photograph of a nearly nude woman holding a sawed-off shotgun, and
the songs within are stark, obscenity-ridden narratives of gang
life. ("Copped an alias, bailed out in an hour or less/I keep a
bank for that don't know about the rest/Copped another piece,
hit the dark streets/ Rollin' once again, fuck the damn police!")

Tolerance of Racism

The ways in which rap has been consumed and popularized
speak not of cross-cultural understanding, musical or otherwise,
but of a voyeurism and tolerance of racism in which black and
white are both complicit. . . . The values it instills find their ultimate expression in the ease with which we watch young black
men killing each other: in movies, on records, and on the streets
of cities and towns across the country.

David Samuels, *The New Republic*, November 11, 1991.

Ice-T is frequently accused of glorifying violence. He claims in
his own defense that his music is a realistic portrait of a violent
world desperately in need of change. Similar arguments can be
heard from the rapidly growing number of rappers who espouse
"socially conscious" rap. Many albums now contain at least one
track extolling the virtues of self-help and attacking the evils of
drugs and black-on-black violence, and several groups put a
consistent emphasis on self-help as a means of enhancing racial
pride and breaking the cycle of poverty. Boogie Down Productions' *Ghetto Music: The Blueprint of Hip Hop* is devoted almost
entirely to songs like "You Must Learn," a paean to the importance of teaching black history in the public schools:
Pump my mind with "See Jane run."
See John walk in a hard-core New York?
Come on, now, that's like a chocolate cow,
It doesn't exist, no way, no how.
It seems to me that in a school that's ebony,
African history should be pumped up steadily.
But it's not—and this has got to stop.

"See Spot run? Run, get Spot!"
Insulting to a black mentality,
A black way of life or a jet-black family.

Farrakhan

Unfortunately there is sometimes more to "self-help" than meets the eye. Boogie Down Productions' first album, *By Any Means Necessary*, took its title from a speech by Malcolm X, a figure greatly esteemed by rappers, and another figure held in high regard in certain rap quarters is Malcolm's successor as chief spokesman for the Black Muslim community, Louis Farrakhan.

Among rappers, to speak of Louis Farrakhan is to speak of Public Enemy, winner of the 1988 *Village Voice* critics' poll and the most celebrated and controversial of all rap groups. Spike Lee brought Public Enemy to the attention of the general public when he featured its recording "Fight the Power" in his movie *Do the Right Thing*. The members of Public Enemy all belong to the Nation of Islam, the black Muslim sect led by Farrakhan; members of the Fruit of Islam, the paramilitary wing of the Nation of Islam, provide on-stage security at Public Enemy concerts. "Bring the Noise," one of Public Enemy's popular numbers, contains the lines "Farrakhan's a prophet and I think you ought to listen to/What he can say to you, what you ought to do." Other tracks on the group's latest album, *It Takes a Nation of Millions to Hold Us Back*, contain explicit references to "black nationalism" and to the Black Muslim demonology familiar to readers of *The Autobiography of Malcolm X*:

To those that disagree, it causes static
For the original Black Asiatic man
Cream of the earth
And was here first
And some devils prevent this from being known
But you check out the books they own
Even Masons they know it
But refuse to show it—yo
But it's proven and fact . . .

The pro-Farrakhan sentiments of Public Enemy were not widely noticed until the Washington *Times* ran its interview with the group's "minister of information," one Professor Griff, in 1989. The *Village Voice* later published extended excerpts from this interview, and other newspapers too began to report that Professor Griff had called Jews "wicked" and had blamed them for "the majority of wickedness that goes on across the globe." In fact, he had much more to say on the subject:

> How come we don't talk about how the Jews finance these experiments on AIDS with black people in South Africa? How come we don't talk about those things? . . .

150

[The Jews] *have* to keep black people in check in America. That's wicked. They have to say Qaddafi is a hater; they have to say Farrakhan is a hater; they have to say the Ayatollah Khomeini is just a religious fanatic; they have to say Idi Amin kills his own people. . . . Personally speaking, these men I admire. . . .

Is it a coincidence that the Jews run the jewelry business, and its named *jew*-elry? No coincidence. Is it a coincidence to you that probably the gold from this ring was brought up out of South Africa, and that the Jews have a tight grip on our brothers in South Africa? . . .

[The Jews] have a history of killing black men. What am I supposed to fear? I fear no one but Allah. I fear God alone. So the Jews can come against me. They can send the IRS after me. They can send their faggot little hit men.

Asked by David Mills of the *Times* for evidence of these accusations, Professor Griff cited Henry Ford's anti-Semitic tract, *The International Jew*, plus a book circulated by the Nation of Islam called *The Secret Relationship Between Blacks and Jews*, and "a series of tapes" by "a brother by the name of Steve Cokely." Cokely, then an adviser to the mayor of Chicago, claimed in 1988 that 300 Jewish doctors were inoculating blacks with the AIDS virus.

Accusations

The *Village Voice* story was published on June 20. The next day, Professor Griff was "fired" from Public Enemy by Chuck D, the group's leader and chief rapper, who called a press conference to apologize to "anyone who might have been offended by Griff's remarks." A week later, Def Jam Recordings, the rap division of CBS Records and Public Enemy's record label, announced that the group was "disbanding for an indefinite period of time."

By August 10, however, Public Enemy had already announced its "reorganization," with Professor Griff rehired under the title of "supreme allied chief of community relations." A number of Jewish groups reacted heatedly to the news. Said Rabbi Abraham Cooper of the Simon Wiesenthal Foundation: "Imagine if there was a country-music group in which one of the members was an open member of the Ku Klux Klan, repeating all the slanders against blacks, Jews, and Vietnamese boat people. How long would he last in the music community?" In fact, reaction within the music community was tepid at best; Russell Simmons, president of Def Jam Recordings, told David Mills that the members of Public Enemy were "ideological idiots" but added irrelevantly that "I listen to Frank Sinatra, too, but I don't listen to him for ideology."

In December, Def Jam released a new Public Enemy single, "Welcome to the Terrordome," which includes a reference by

Chuck D to the controversy over Professor Griff's Washington *Times* interview: "Crucifixion ain't no fiction/ So-called chosen, frozen/Apologies made to whoever pleases/Still, they got me like Jesus." On December 28, a letter was sent by the Anti-Defamation League of B'nai Brith to CBS Records protesting "Welcome to the Terrordome" on the grounds that it "contains blatantly anti-Semitic lyrics, including the repulsive and historically discredited charge of deicide on the part of the Jews. . . ." In response, Chuck D told the Washington *Post* that the passage in question was not anti-Semitic, and dismissed criticism of "Welcome to the Terrordome" as "paranoiac.". . .

Bigotry

Many people who know Chuck D, including Rabbi Cooper, maintain that he is not personally anti-Semitic. I should note, too, that I have failed to encounter any examples of directly anti-Semitic lyrics or public statements by rappers other than the ones made by Professor Griff in the Washington *Times* and by Chuck D in "Welcome to the Terrordome." But the anti-Semitism in those two instances is blatant and unmistakable; and it is not the only pernicious doctrine circulating in the world of rap. Russell Simmons says that "Chuck D is very, very important to a lot of black kids in America—he's contributed so much to black youth, to the growth of black awareness and black pride." The question naturally arises: what kind of awareness? What kind of pride?

One example can be found in a statement Chuck D made in August during an interview with David Hinckley of the New York *Daily News:*

> You have to tell people why, for example, you see so many drug dealers in the black community and not in the white. You explain who's *behind* the drug thing, why it's the brothers who are dying. You point out that Jesse Jackson had twice the qualities of any other candidate, but because we have this system where people are judged by their characteristics, he couldn't win. And then you tell kids to stop wanting a gold chain and a fly [stylish] car and get educated—because black people have to take care of themselves and the only way to do it is as a community.

The last sentence of this statement could have come from any one of a dozen rappers advocating black self-help. The preceding sentences are another matter entirely. They allude to the theory, increasingly popular among urban blacks, that there is a conspiracy by powerful whites to commit "genocide" against the black community. In fact, more or less explicit talk of genocide is not uncommon among "socially conscious" rappers. In their songs, policemen kill blacks casually and deliberately, and the federal government, usually personified by Ronald Reagan or, more recently, George Bush, is the mortal enemy of all blacks. White racism, one and indivisible, is the principle of American social organization; all blacks are its perpetual objects; white and black America are in a state of de-facto war.

What the black response should be to these "facts" is the subject of a recent recording by Ice-T, "This One's for Me":

Griff is my man, I don't care what he said
You know what I'm saying?
And I ain't gonna let them go out like that. . . .
Anybody out there got problems with Public Enemy,
Come talk to me. . . .
I gotta speak my mind, it's time to unload
On this so-called government we got
I lied like them, I think I'd get shot
They sell drugs to kids and say it's us
And when the cops are crooks, who can you trust? . . .
Selling drugs is straight-up genocide
They're gonna laugh while we all die.

Critics of rap are fairly quick to decry "sexism" in recordings like Slick Rick's "Treat Her Like a Prostitute." But when it comes to such raps as "This One's for Me" or "Welcome to the Terrordome," many of these critics are even quicker to mount the nearest fence. Peter Watrous, who reviewed a concert by Public Enemy for the New York *Times*, noted that it opened with a lecture by Professor Griff claiming that the U.S. and Soviet governments were jointly responsible for the AIDS epidemic (admittedly, a slight improvement on blaming the Jews). To this and comparable statements, Watrous's response was that "while the group's political discourse is undigested at best and secondary to the urgency of their overall sound, it at least opens the always necessary debate about racism." So it does—although not the kind of racism Watrous seems to have in mind.

Periodical Bibliography

The following articles have been selected to supplement the diverse views presented in this chapter.

Danny Alexander   "American Apartheid: A Native American Activist Visits New York to Embrace the Hip-Hop Nation," *The Source*, February 1993. Available from *The Source*, 594 Broadway, Suite 510, New York, NY 10012.

P. Biskind   "Mind Rot," *Premiere*, August 1992.

Dan Charnas   "A Gangsta's World View," *The Source*, Summer 1990.

Theresa L. Ebert   "The Politics of the Outrageous," *Women's Review of Books*, October 1991.

Free Inquiry   "Secular Humanism and Traditional Values," Fall 1992.

Andrew Greeley   "Like a Catholic: Madonna's Challenge to Her Church," *America*, April 13, 1989.

Robin D.G. Kelley   "Straight from Underground," *The Nation*, June 8,1992.

John Leland   "Cube on Thin Ice," *Newsweek*, December 2, 1991.

Joe Maxwell   "The New Hollywood Watchdogs," *Christianity Today*, April 27, 1992.

Carolyn J. Mooney   "Camille Paglia, Academic Guerrilla," *Chronicle of Higher Education*, April 1, 1992.

Newsweek   "The New Voyeurism: Madonna and the Selling of Sex," November 2, 1992.

Alex Patterson   "Penetration, Urination, and Gratuitous Vomiting," *Film Comment*, May/June 1991.

Dennis Polkow   "Rock Meets Classical," *Musical America*, January/February 1991.

Edward Rothstein   "Roll Over Beethoven: The New Musical Correctness and Its Mistakes," *The New Republic*, February 4, 1991.

David Samuels   "The Rap on Rap," *The New Republic*, November 11, 1991.

Joan Tarshis   "YoYo: Rapping Back," *Ms.*, July/August 1991.

James Q. Wilson   "The Family Values Debate," *Commentary*, April 1993.

4 CHAPTER

Should Government Enforce Cultural Values?

CULTURE WARS

Chapter Preface

The debate about the proper relationship between government and culture is an ancient one, as old as civilization itself. Among the Greeks, Plato contended in his *Republic* and other works that political power should be expressed through an exclusive class of rulers he called Guardians. This class, he believed, should constitute a natural aristocracy (rule of the "best") whose education would be carefully protected from the degenerative tendencies of democracy (rule of the "people"). Since the Guardians were the "best," they should study only what was truly excellent—what might be considered "high culture"—in ideas, art, advanced mathematics, and philosophy. Plato contended that strict censorship should prevail over his young guardians; he did not particularly care what the lower classes did for entertainment.

Throughout much of subsequent European history, Plato's model was often followed, insofar as high culture became the preserve of aristocratic ruling classes who also held political power. In America, through the dramatic success of our revolution, culture became democratized: "Yankee Doodle" made fun of the British lords, and the First Amendment made criticism of all governments freely legal. In the nineteenth century, public education brought the skills of literacy and science to masses of citizens. At a time of national crisis in the 1930s, in the midst of the Great Depression, the federal government subsidized large-scale programs for art, theater, and literature, thus establishing a precedent for outright public support of culture. In the 1960s, such support was renewed in the form of the Public Broadcasting Service and the National Endowment for the Arts. In order to protect these agencies from undue political pressure, a system of professional peer review was devised, which meant that grants and projects were judged not by bureaucrats, but by artists and video producers themselves.

In the mid- and late-1980s, the fragile consensus for federal support of the arts was broken by controversies concerning the homoerotic photography of Robert Mapplethorpe, grants for this and similar projects from the National Endowment for the Arts, and controlling the lyrics of rock music. Should our young people's interest in rock somehow be controlled by society? What right to public support should homoerotic art have, if any? The authors of this chapter debate the competing values of public morality, artistic quality, and artistic freedom.

156

"What is taking place is yet another perverse manipulation of the public by the contemporary art establishment."

The National Endowment for the Arts Should Be More Discriminating

Frederick Hart

In the following viewpoint, Frederick Hart contends that the historic mission of art is to be a "form of service," as it was in Renaissance Italy. The antisocial bohemianism of the arts today might have made some sense in the nineteenth century, he says, but it has now degenerated into a cynical attack on fundamental social values. Artists claim the right to be contemptuous of public morality, according to Hart, but they should not also demand substantial financial support from that same public. Hart is a member of the Commission of Fine Arts in Washington, D.C., and the sculptor of the statue depicting Vietnam veterans that stands next to the war memorial.

As you read, consider the following questions:

1. Why, according to Hart, do those in the "art world" consider themselves to be "free spirits"? Who does Hart call the "troglodytes"?
2. What, according to the author, are examples of "sacred public sentiments"?
3. How does Hart define "art . . . rededicating itself to life rather than art"?

Frederick Hart, "Contemporary Art Is Perverted Art," *The Washington Post*, August 22, 1989. Reprinted with permission.

The air is becoming suffocatingly pungent with the incense of pious indignation from the art world concerning Congress' reaction to the way the National Endowment for the Arts is spending taxpayers' money.

What is taking place is yet another perverse manipulation of the public by the contemporary art establishment. The public, through its instrument, Congress, has reacted to the baiting and taunting of its sense of decency by the art world through its instrument, the NEA. Underneath its outrage, the art world can barely contain its secret delight at this publicity bonanza featuring a heroic scenario of free spirits versus troglodytes.

Deliberate Contempt

What eludes the public is the current philosophy and practice of art, which not only delights in but thrives on a belief system of deliberate contempt for the public. In order to understand this, you have to understand the values of art today and how contemporary art is intellectually packaged for the marketplace. To grasp this is also to grasp the sorry moral condition of art today and how this is shriveling art, making it less and less a meaningful endeavor.

Since the beginnings of bohemianism in art in the late 19th century, rejection by the public has become the traditional hallmark of what comes to be regarded as great art. An offended public is a critical necessity for the attainment of credentials by any artist. The idea that art and artist must be initially misunderstood and rejected has become doctrine in the mythology of great art, and consequently it has become one of the primary criteria in evaluating the historical importance of a given artist. The art world embraced this fable in the late 19th century and has been running hard with it ever since.

There is, however, a critical difference between then and now. Life in the late 19th century was heavily regimented by strict societal mores: the public expression of emotion and sexuality was severely repressed. When art and literature broke through those layers of repression, people were offended, outraged and ill at ease about the truths they discovered about themselves. But we live in a different world. Today, "repression" is a bad word. Nothing is ever, ever repressed. Everything is discussed, analyzed and ventilated by people ranging from Phil Donahue in the morning to Larry King at night, day in and day out. It's gotten damned hard if not almost impossible to offend anyone anymore.

But art persists. Every artist worth his salt yearns to create works of art that are (mistakenly perceived, of course) so offensive, so insulting to the public as to earn him a clear judgment of genius for his success at being misunderstood.

It has become the intense pastime of contemporary art to pursue controversy, the bigger the better, as a form of art. But the artist has had to reach farther and deeper to find some new twist with which to offend. A simple-minded little sophomoric gimmick of making people walk on the flag to make a cute point arouses vast passion and national controversy—for which artist and art world pat each other on the back.

What is really going on is the cynical aggrandizement of art and artist at the expense of sacred public sentiments—profound sentiments embodied by symbols, such as the flag or the crucifix, which the public has a right and a duty to treasure and protect.

Art and Society

When one looks back at the majestic sweep of art in history and its awesome and magnificent accomplishments, how nasty and midget like are so many of the products and so much of the philosophy of contemporary art by comparison. Once, art served society rather than biting at its heels while demanding unequivocal financial support. Once, under the banner of beauty and order, art was a rich and meaningful embellishment of life, embracing—not desecrating—its ideals, its aspirations and its values.

Not so today.

No Sense of Responsibility

The recent attacks have brought out all the old clichés about the value of art as "an essential component of our civilization," the "conscience of society," etc. And yet any casual gallery or contemporary art museum survey reveals that the majority of work on display has less to do with the expression of eternal or difficult truths than it does with fitting into the categories of high-priced collectibles or light entertainment. For decades the art world has resolutely separated itself from any sense of responsibility toward the social world, which makes the humanistic terms with which it defends itself now more than a little suspect.

Eleanor Heartney, *Sculpture*, January/February 1990.

Look about you. The artlessness of contemporary life has come about because of a breakdown in the fundamental philosophy of art and who it is created for. The flaw is not with a public that refuses to nourish the arts. Rather it is with a practice of art that refuses to nourish the public. The public has been so bullied intellectually by the proponents of contemporary art that it has wearily resigned itself to just about any idiocy that is put before it and calls itself art. But the common man has his limits, and they are reached when some of these things emerge from the sanctuary of the padded cells of galleries and museums and are put in public places, where the public is forced to live with them and pay for them.

If one visited a town or a city in Renaissance Italy, the motive of art and its resulting products would come off entirely differently. Art was not then thought of as an end in itself but as another form of service. When the Italian peasant looked about, he saw an array of dedicated embellishments from his church to his public buildings, fountains and plazas. The artwork, which was exquisitely created, embraced his values, his religious beliefs, his history, his aspirations and his ideals. It was meant to give enrichment through its artistry but, more important, to give purpose through its meaning. It was, as Dante called sculpture, "visible speech." It was not created for art's sake but for his sake.

The measure of achievement in art was determined by the degree to which that art was considered ennobling. Art and society had achieved a wonderful responsibility for each other. Art summarized, with masterful visual eloquence born of a sense of beauty, the striving of civilization to find order and purpose in the universe. This service to truth was more important than the endeavor of art itself. And it was this dedication to service that gave art its moral authority.

This moral authority is the critical element by which a society regards art either as an essential and meaningful part of life, as in Renaissance Italy or, as today, a superfluous bit of fluff, mainly indulged in by a small snobbish minority. Art is regarded by contemporary society much the same way architects now regard art—not as an essence, but as a high-rent amenity.

The most touching and noble impulse toward "visible speech" in recent times was the short-lived creation of the Statue of Democracy in Tiananmen Square. Naively executed, it was nonetheless a wonderful display of the unique ability of art to embody and enhance concisely and movingly a deeply felt public yearning for an ideal of a just society. The profound meaning the statue had for tens of millions of people gives the art a value and moral authority of profound significance.

The Nobility of Ideas

In ancient Greece, which generated 2,500 years of Western art, there existed no distinction between aesthetics and ethics in the judgment of a work of art. Works of art achieved greatness by embodying great ideas, as well as by sheer mastery of the medium. The inspiration and the motivation for that mastery were in the nobility of the ideas pursued.

It is the contemporary renunciation of the moral responsibility of art that is the source of the recent hostilities between art and public. The cutback of funds by Congress is a graphic display of the public's declining conviction of the importance of art, caused by a self-absorbed art that has lost all sense of obligation to the public good and the betterment of man. It is possible to live without art, and if the nourishment provided by art continues to be so nauseating, life without art will become, for some, desirable.

If art is to flourish in the 21st century, it must renew its moral authority by philosophically and fundamentally rededicating itself to life rather than art. Art must again touch our lives, our fears and cares. It must evoke our dreams and give hope to the darkness.

*"When losses are suffered in public arenas,
people for whom controversial or minority images
are salient and affirming suffer a real defeat."*

The National Endowment for the Arts Does Not Need to Be More Discriminating

Carole S. Vance

Carole S. Vance is a professor of anthropology at Columbia University and frequently speaks at conferences on censorship and related subjects. In the following viewpoint, Vance contends that attacks on the NEA are unjustified. She believes that the NEA serves a valuable function in supporting a number of arts, not just the controversial few that have received so much attention. Vance calls for a courageous and forthright defense of "controversial" content in contemporary art and believes that public funding remains essential.

As you read, consider the following questions:

1. How have fundamentalists "modernized their rhetoric" in the current attack on art, according to the author? Why have they done so?
2. Why, contends Vance, are symbols so important in culture? Why do people dispute so fiercely about symbols and their treatment in art?
3. How, in Vance's view, are distinctions between public and private "false"? How is this relevant to her argument in defense of artistic freedom?

Carole S. Vance, "The War on Culture," *Art in America*, September 1989. Reprinted with permission.

Fundamentalists and conservatives are now directing mass-based symbolic mobilizations against "high culture." Previously, their efforts had focused on popular culture—the attack on rock music led by Tipper Gore, the protests against *The Last Temptation of Christ* and the Meese Commission's war against pornography. Conservative and neoconservative intellectuals have also lamented the allegedly liberal bias of the university and the dilution of the classic literary canon by including "inferior" works by minority, female and gay authors, but these complaints have been made in books, journals and conferences, and have scarcely generated thousands of letters to Congress. Previous efforts to change the direction of the NEA [National Endowment for the Arts] had been made through institutional and bureaucratic channels—by appointing more conservative members to its governing body, the National Council on the Arts, by selecting a more conservative chair and in some cases by overturning grant decisions made by professional panels. Although antagonism to Eastern elites and upper-class culture has been a thread within fundamentalism, the NEA controversy marks the first time that this emotion has been tapped in mass political action.

A Cultural Revolution

Conservative columnist Patrick Buchanan sounded the alarm for this populist attack in a *Washington Times* column, calling for "a cultural revolution in the '90s as sweeping as the political revolution in the '80s." Here may lie a clue to this new strategy: the Reagan political revolution has peaked, and with both legislatures under Democratic control, additional conservative gains on social issues through electoral channels seem unlikely. Under these conditions, the slower and more time-consuming—though perhaps more effective—method of changing public opinion and taste may be the best available option. For conservatives and fundamentalists, the arts community plays a significant role in setting standards and shaping public values: Buchanan writes, "The decade has seen an explosion of anti-American, anti-Christian, and nihilist 'art'. . . . [Many museums] now feature exhibits that can best be described as cultural trash," and "as in public television and public radio, a tiny clique, out of touch with America's traditional values, has wormed its way into control of the arts bureaucracy." In an analogy chillingly reminiscent of Nazi cultural metaphors, Buchanan writes, "As with our rivers and lakes, we need to clean up our culture: for it is a well from which we must all drink. Just as a poisoned land will yield up poisonous fruits, so a polluted culture, left to fester and stink, can destroy a nation's soul." Let the citizens be warned: "We should not subsidize decadence." Amid such archaic language of moral pollution

163

and degeneracy, it was not surprising that Mapplethorpe's gay and erotic images were at the center of controversy.

The second new element in the right's mass mobilization against the NEA and high culture has been its rhetorical disavowal of censorship per se and the cultivation of an artfully crafted distinction between absolute censorship and the denial of public funding. Senator Alphonse D'Amato, for example, claimed, "This matter does not involve freedom of artistic expression—it does involve the question whether American taxpayers should be forced to support such trash." In the battle for public opinion, "censorship" is a dirty word to mainstream audiences, and hard for conservatives to shake off because their recent battles to control school books, libraries and curricula have earned them reputations as ignorant book-burners. By using this hairsplitting rhetoric, conservatives can now happily disclaim any interest in censorship, and merely suggest that no public funds be used for "offensive" or "indecent" materials. Conservatives had employed the "no public funds" argument before to deny federal funding for Medicaid abortions since 1976 and explicit safe-sex education for AIDS more recently. Fundamentalists have attempted to modernize their rhetoric in other social campaigns, too—antiabortionists borrow civil rights terms to speak about the "human rights" of the fetus, and antiporn zealots experiment with replacing their language of sin and lust with phrases about the "degradation of women" borrowed from antipornography feminism. In all cases, these incompatible languages have an uneasy coexistence. But modernized rhetoric cannot disguise the basic, censorious impulse which strikes out at NEA public funding precisely because it is a significant source of arts money, not a trivial one.

NEA's Reach

NEA funding permeates countless art institutions, schools and community groups, often making the difference between survival and going under; it also supports many individual artists. That NEA funds have in recent years been allocated according to formulas designed to achieve more democratic distribution—not limited to elite art centers or well-known artists—makes their impact all the more significant. A requirement that NEA-funded institutions and artists conform to a standard of "public taste," even in the face of available private funds, would have a profound impact. One obvious by-product would be installing the fiction of a singular public with a universally shared taste and the displacement of a diverse public composed of may constituencies with different tastes. In addition, the mingling of NEA and private funds, so typical in many institutions and exhibitions, would mean that NEA standards would spill over to the private sector, which is separate more in theory than in practice. Although NEA might fund only part of a project, its standards would prevail, since noncompliance would result in loss of funds.

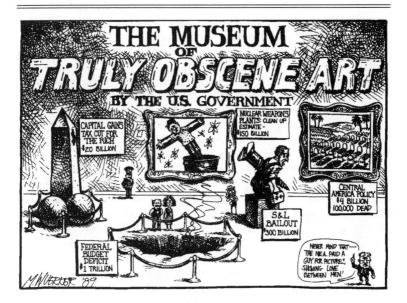

© Matt Wuerker. Reprinted with permission.

No doubt the continuous contemplation of the standards of public taste that should obtain in publicly funded projects—continuous, since these can never be known with certainty—will itself increase self-censorship and caution across the board. There has always been considerable self-censorship in the art world when it comes to sexual images, and the evidence indicates that it is increasing: reports circulate about curators now examining their collections anew with an eye toward "disturbing" material that might arouse public ire, and increased hesitation to mount new exhibitions that contain unconventional material. In all these ways, artists have recognized the damage done by limiting the types of images that can be funded by public monies.

But more importantly, the very distinction between public and private is a false one, because the boundaries between these spheres are very permeable. Feminist scholarship has shown how the most seemingly personal and private decisions—having a baby, for example—are affected by a host of public laws and policies, ranging from available tax benefits to health services to day care. In the past century in America and England, major changes in family form, sexuality and gender arrangements have occurred in a complex web spanning public and private domains, which even historians are hard put to separate. In struggles for social change, both reformers and traditionalists know that changes in personal life are intimately linked to changes in public domains—not only through legal regulation, but also through information, images and even access to physical space available in public arenas.

This is to say that what goes on in the public sphere is of vital importance for both the arts and for political culture. Because American traditions of publicly supported culture are limited by the innate conservatism of corporate sponsors and by the reduction of individual patronage following changes in the tax laws, relegating controversial images and art work to private philanthropy confines them to a frail and easily influenced source of support. Even given the NEA's history of bureaucratic interference, it is paradoxically public funding—insulated from the day-to-day interference of politicians and special-interest groups that the right wing would now impose—that permits the possibility of a heterodox culture. Though we might reject the overly literal connection conservatives like to make between images and action ("When teenagers read sex education, they go out and have sex"), we too know that diversity in images and expression in the public sector nurtures and sustains diversity in private life. When losses are suffered in public arenas, people for whom controversial or minority images are salient and affirming suffer a real defeat. Defending private rights—to behavior, to images, to information—is difficult without a publicly formed and visible community. People deprived of images become demoralized and isolated, and they become increasingly vulnerable to attacks on their private expression of nonconformity, which are inevitable once sources of public solidarity and resistance have been eliminated.

For these reasons, the desire to eliminate symbols, images and ideas they do not like from public space is basic to contemporary conservatives' and fundamentalists' politics about sexuality, gender and the family. On the one hand, this behavior may signal weakness, in that conservatives no longer have the power to directly control, for example, sexual behavior, and must content themselves with controlling a proxy, images of sexual behavior. The attack on Mapplethorpe's images, some of them gay, some sadomasochistic, can be understood in this light. Indeed, the savage critique of his photographs permitted a temporary revival of a vocabulary—"perverted, filth, trash"—that was customarily used against gays but has become unacceptable in mainstream political discourse, a result of sexual liberalization that conservatives hate. On the other hand, the attack on images, particularly "difficult" images in the public domain, may be the most effective point of cultural intervention now—particularly given the evident difficulty liberals have in mounting a strong and unambivalent response and given the way changes in public climate can be translated back to changes in legal rights—as, for example, in the erosion of support for abortion rights, where the image of the fetus has become central in the debate, erasing the image of the woman.

Because symbolic mobilizations and moral panics often leave in their wake residues of law and policy that remain in force long after the hysteria has subsided, the fundamentalist attack on art and images requires a broad and vigorous response that goes beyond appeals to free speech. Free expression is a necessary principle in these debates, because of the steady protection it offers to all images, but it cannot be the only one. To be effective and not defensive, the art community needs to employ its interpretive skills to unmask the modernized rhetoric conservatives use to justify their traditional agenda, as well as to deconstruct the "difficult" images fundamentalists choose to set their campaigns in motion. Despite their uncanny intuition for culturally disturbing material, their focus on images also contains many sleights of hand (Do photographs of nude children necessarily equal child pornography?), and even displacement, which we need to examine. Images we would allow to remain "disturbing" and unconsidered put us anxiously on the defensive and undermine our own response. In addition to defending free speech, it is essential to address why certain images are being attacked—Serrano's crucifix for mocking the excesses of religious exploitation (a point evidently not lost on the televangelists and syndicated preachers who promptly assailed his "blasphemy") and Mapplethorpe's photographs for making minority sexual subcultures visible. If we are always afraid to offer a public defense of sexual images, then even in our rebuttal we have granted the right wing its most basic premise: sexuality is shameful and discrediting. It is not enough to defend the principle of free speech, while joining in denouncing the image, as some in the art world have done.

The fundamentalist attack on images and the art world must be recognized not as an improbable and silly outburst of Yahooism, but as a systematic part of a right-wing political program to restore traditional social arrangements and reduce diversity. The right wing is deeply committed to symbolic politics, both in using symbols to mobilize public sentiment and in understanding that, because images do stand in for and motivate social change, the arena of representation is a real ground for struggle. A vigorous defense of art and images begins from this insight.

> *"American taxpayers are furious that their hard-earned money can be spent on so-called art that is obscene, indecent, blasphemous and racist."*

The National Endowment for the Arts Should Be Defunded

Dana Rohrabacher

As a Republican member of the U.S. House of Representatives from California, Dana Rohrabacher has been outspoken in his attack on the NEA. In the following viewpoint, taken from a speech to the House in 1989 at the height of a debate over whether the NEA should have given grants to support Robert Mapplethorpe's homoerotic photographs, Rohrabacher argued that since the NEA has often supported such "trash," government funding for the agency should entirely cease. His proposal did not pass, but his contribution to the debate forcefully expressed the conservative viewpoint.

As you read, consider the following questions:

1. What evidence of obscenity does Rohrabacher cite to support his argument?
2. What distinction does Rohrabacher make between sponsorship and censorship?
3. Would the author's amendment have any impact on obscene art produced outside the auspices of the NEA?

Excerpted from Dana Rohrabacher's statement to the U.S. House of Representatives, September 13, 1989.

Mr. Speaker, American taxpayers are furious that their hard-earned money can be spent on so-called art that is obscene, indecent, blasphemous and racist. . . .

Mr. Speaker, a few weeks ago, I stood before the House and offered a simple amendment to the Interior appropriations bill. My amendment would have struck all Government funding of the National Endowment for the Arts.

Those who truly oppose Government control of the arts should oppose Government funding of the arts. Money for the arts should be left with the people, rather than taxed away, so they can make their own free determination as to what art they will or will not support, rather than giving that power to the state. But if the Government does tax away our people's hard-earned money in the name of supporting the arts, at the very least, standards should be set so that those funds are not used to subsidize obscenity or indecency, or used to denigrate someone's religion, or race, or sex.

Opponents of my amendment suggest that establishing standards for the use of taxpayers' money is a form of censorship. What kind of cockamamie logic is that? The question is sponsorship, not censorship. At a time of high deficit spending, when it is difficult to provide funds for the health needs of our elderly and for prenatal care, spending the taxpayers' dollars on art is itself questionable. Spending it on obscene or indecent art, or art that insults one's religion, is outrageous.

There has been a great deal of posturing on this issue. One wonders how many of those who are aggressively opposing the setting of these standards would be doing so, if it had been a photo of Martin Luther King or a symbol of the Jewish faith that had been submerged in a bottle of urine at taxpayers' expense.

Now we hear that the Helms language, which passed by the Senate without opposition, is too broad, unclear, a threat to legitimate art and freedom of expression. This strawman argument is being used to oppose the setting of any standards. The language of this amendment is direct, clear and understandable. . . .

American Taxpayers' Concern

If there are some in this hall who have trouble understanding this clear and direct language, I am certain there are voters around this country who are willing to explain it to them in the next election. Americans believe in freedom of speech, but let there be no doubt, the American people do not want their tax dollars spent on obscenity and indecency or for denigrating Christianity or any other religion. . . .

Yes, the NEA could still sponsor submerging photos of myself or Senator Helms or any other politician, but they could not use our tax dollars to put a crucifix of Jesus Christ in a bottle of urine, or denigrate any other religion; and do not tell the American people that they are bigoted, or tyrannical for insisting that standards be set so their hard-earned tax dollars are not used for such trash and mean spirited invective against race, religion, sex or handicap.

Government Out of the Arts

It is more than a little disingenuous for arts sponsors and presenters to believe they can drink at the federal funding faucet and not, at some point, be held accountable. The alternative? Perhaps the only solution is to get the government out of the arts business altogether.

David Hudson, *Kansas City Star*, March 27, 1992.

Time magazine said that had Federal authorities chosen to do so, they could have prosecuted Robert Mapplethorpe for child pornography. Other projects sponsored by the NEA have included drawings of homosexual orgies, bestiality, and a Statue of Liberty turned into a transvestite, complete with male sex organs.

Why in the world are we permitting Federal tax dollars to be used to finance such trash? How in the name of representative government can anyone oppose the setting of standards to prevent this obscene misuse of tax dollars?

The censorship argument is without merit. Artists can do whatever they want on their own time and with their own dime. We, on the other hand, have a responsibility to see that tax dollars are spent for the betterment of our country.

"The issue ... is very simple ... whether we in the U.S. Senate should attempt to make definitions of what we consider to be suitable art."

The National Endowment for the Arts Should Not Be Defunded

John Danforth

As the senior senator from Missouri, John Danforth has become a prominent spokesman for moderate conservatism. In the following viewpoint taken from a speech to the Senate, Danforth addresses the Helms amendment which would have prohibited support for art which denigrates the objects or beliefs of the adherents of a particular religion or nonreligion. Danforth argues that such a law would be impossible to enforce fairly, since art and literature are by their nature somewhat controversial at times, and furthermore, in any society some people are likely to find almost anything offensive.

As you read, consider the following questions:

1. What is the author's judgment of the artistic exhibits displayed in the Senate as examples of obscene art?
2. How do Danforth's examples of "objectionable" art represent differing concepts of religion, sex, age, and national origin?
3. Why does Danforth say that the Helms amendment is "not just about Mapplethorpe; it is also about Shakespeare"?

Excerpted from John Danforth's statement to the U.S. Senate, September 29, 1989.

I have unfortunately had the opportunity to look very briefly at the exhibits that the Senator from North Carolina has brought to the floor and everything that has been said about them is true. These are gross. These are terrible. These are totally indefensible. I do not think they are art.

However I do not believe that the issue before us tonight is whether we like or do not like these pictures. I do not like them and my guess is that not a single resident of my State would like them. They would not like the idea of the Government paying for them. I am sorry Government did pay for them.

That is not the issue before us. The issue is very simple: . . . What is suitable art? And the issue before the Senate is very simple, and it is whether we in the U.S. Senate should attempt to make definitions of what we consider to be suitable art.

Maybe there should not be any National Endowment for the Arts. Maybe the Government should never be in the business of making judgments of taste, because that is what the NEA does. I think that is an arguable position. But the question is not whether the NEA should do it or not do it. We have already decided that the NEA is in that business.

The question is whether we in the Congress of the United States should try to establish some criteria by which we define what is or is not suitable art. That is what the Senator from North Carolina does by his amendment. His amendment does not say that the Mapplethorpe exhibition is pornography and it should not be funded. He does not say that. He goes much more broadly than that. . . .

He goes much more broadly than that in the terms of his amendment, and I want to read a couple paragraphs because we have been focusing on obscenity and I think everybody knows that obscenity has been a problem for the Supreme Court of the United States. But he also says in paragraph 2 that the amendment covers material which denigrates the object or beliefs of the adherents of a particular religion or nonreligion.

Too Broad a Definition

Mr. President, consider what that means: Material which denigrates the object or beliefs of the adherents of a particular religion or nonreligion.

Does it denigrate the object of a religion to portray Christ as a clown? Well, the musical "Godspell" did just that. It portrayed Christ as a clown. Could it be found by some administrator that the portrayal of Christ as a clown denigrates the object of somebody's religion? Of course it could.

"Godspell" probably would be covered by the breadth of this amendment.

How about a portrayal of Christ as a wild animal? Would that portrayal denigrate a person's religion? Well, C.S. Lewis did that in "The Lion, the Witch and the Wardrobe." It was a book about Christianity and the Christ figure was a lion and some administrator, some bureaucrat could have said that denigrates a person's religion. C.S. Lewis spent his academic and literary life describing his religious beliefs which were very, very profound beliefs.

© Matt Wuerker. Reprinted with permission.

How about in the world of music? Could it be said that the beliefs of the Quaker faith are denigrated by "Onward Christian Soldiers Marching as to War"?

And then how about the question of race. I remember from my own part of the country, "Tom Sawyer" and "Huckleberry Finn." There have been those throughout the last number of decades who have tried for one reason or another to get "Tom Sawyer" and "Huckleberry Finn" off of the shelves of our schools.

This amendment would say that "Tom Sawyer" would not have qualified for an NEA grant and "Huckleberry Finn" because it could be argued that they denigrated an individual, namely Nigger Jim, as he was called according to his race.

Or how about creed? Can we think of anything in the annals

173

of literature that denigrates an individual because of his religion? How about the "Merchant of Venice"? How about William Shakespeare himself? Would that be covered by this amendment? I think it would be. This amendment is not just about Mapplethorpe. It is also about Shakespeare.

And in our own time in American literature Alice Walker's great little book, "The Color Purple," made into a movie, clearly denigrates men.

And this amendment says that material that denigrates or reviles a person on the basis of sex falls within the parameters. I take it that "The Color Purple" would not have qualified for an NEA grant.

How about age? I do not remember the name of the book, but I do remember that Bill Cosby, the famous comedian, wrote a book about kids. It is a spoof of children, and his television programs are always doing that. And I take it that those programs and that book denigrate people on the basis of age.

Then there is national origin which is also covered material that denigrates or reviles on the basis of national origin. Perhaps "The Godfather." The head of Paramount Theaters was visiting with me recently. I said, "What is the greatest movie you ever made?" He said, "The two Godfather movies taken together, absolutely the essence of American art" and it would be covered by this amendment.

I am not for Mapplethorpe. I am sick that a dollar of taxpayer money went to pay for this kind of junk. I am sick about it. I could just see the faces of the people of Sedalia, or Cabool, or Mountain Grove, MO, if they were told that they had to pay for this. It truly is outlandish. That is not the issue.

The issue is: How good are we at defining whether something is suitable art or not-suitable art and how do we draw those definitions? And should we really write definitions on the floor of the Senate which cover "Godspell," and "Tom Sawyer," and the "Merchant of Venice," and "The Color Purple," and "The Godfather?" Mr. President, I think the answer is no.

"Public broadcasting . . . is no longer the altruistic alternative we were promised."

Public Television Should Reflect Mainstream Values

Robert Dole

In his positions as majority and minority leader of the Republican party in the Senate, Robert Dole of Kansas has been an articulate and witty proponent of midwestern conservatism. In the following viewpoint, he questions continuing tax support for the Corporation for Public Broadcasting, which produces a part of the programming for PBS-TV, on the grounds that the station's executive salaries are exorbitant, it has a narrow geographical distribution of funding support, and that much of its programming is politically and sexually unacceptable.

As you read, consider the following questions:

1. How, according to Dole, does public television's success mean that government support is no longer necessary?
2. How does public TV reflect "big city bias"?
3. What kinds of programs does Dole object to? What would it mean if the "marketplace" took complete control of programming?

Robert Dole, "Time to Review Role of Public TV, Radio," *Kansas City Star*, March 25, 1992. Reprinted with permission.

W_{hy} are taxpayers subsidizing an organization that grosses $100 million a year and has an investment portfolio worth at least another $52 million?

It's a good question, because that's exactly what happens when Congress votes to send your tax dollar to the Children's Television Workshop, the so-called non-profit production company behind "Sesame Street."

Don't get me wrong. We all love Big Bird and the Cookie Monster. But do they really need the $14 million taxpayers gave them in 1991 when "Sesame Street" and its merchandising power are raking in piles of retail cash?

This is just one example of the growing problems in public broadcasting, an effort that was launched 25 years ago with high ideals but that today, after billions of taxpayer dollars, is no longer the altruistic alternative we were promised.

The U.S. Senate has opened debate on future funding for the Corporation for Public Broadcasting (CPB), the umbrella bureaucracy that oversees public television and public radio. CPB is asking Congress to authorize a 50 percent increase in federal funding, a total of $1.1 billion for 1994, 1995 and 1996. In addition, CPB receives advanced funding in the annual congressional appropriations bills.

This kind of full funding two years in advance is almost unprecedented—the National Institutes of Health, the Pentagon and the Department of Education don't get this kind of red carpet treatment, yet some folks are still demanding a free ride through Congress for CPB funding and its 50 percent raise.

How the Money Is Spent

In my view, anytime taxpayers are being asked to dig into their pockets for that kind of money, they have a right to know how it is being spent, and on what. Unfortunately, when it comes to public broadcasting, trying to account for taxpayer dollars usually turns into a wild goose chase.

From the lavish offices of highly paid public TV executives in Los Angeles, New York, Boston and Washington the message seems to be, "We're doing a great job, so don't ask any questions. And by the way, keep that taxpayer money pouring in."

Taking a look at some of their salaries, expenses, benefits, travel and handsome investment portfolios, you can see why they don't want too much sunshine breaking through the cloud cover: $641,000 for the Children's Television Workshop president; $207,000 for its vice president; $309,000 for the executive producer at New York City's public TV station WNET, a station that also pocketed $30 million in public funds; $242,000 for the president of the Los Angeles public TV station KCET, and $2.1 million for public television lobbyists.

Then there is the high-tech satellite network that taxpayers bought public radio and TV several years ago, and then spent $200 million more in 1991 for "replacement, upgrading and maintenance."

Now, the satellite system may make for better news, but taxpayers may go into orbit themselves when they find out that PBS and its affiliated companies and stations seem to be making plenty of money by renting time on its taxpayer-subsidized satellite.

It's another outrageous example of the pure profit side of the supposedly non-profit public broadcasting, the network you are underwriting with tax dollars, the network that wants a 50 percent raise.

Reprinted by permission: Tribune Media Services.

Understand, my concerns are not with our Kansas stations, but rather with elitists on the East and West coasts who control much of the programming.

For example, of the $44 million worth of taxpayer dollars made available for program development for some 341 PBS stations, half of the funding goes to only two stations, WGBH in Boston and WNET in New York. Another $10 million goes to a group of producers affiliated with WNET-TV, to three other stations, and to PBS itself.

No wonder public television reflects big city bias. Just ask yourself, when was the last time you saw a public TV documentary on the family farm, small towns, or anything else in mainstream America?

Speaking of documentaries, the CPB added another taxpayer-funded entity to its empire in 1989—the Independent Television Service (ITVS), a would-be "alternative programming" commission. But despite its claims that these alternative programs were urgently needed on public television, ITVS spent the past years burning up $1.5 million on travel expenses, consultants and salaries and did not produce one second of programming.

After pressure from watchdog groups, ITVS finally announced 25 grant winners, and guess what, 15 of them are in New York and five in California. The ITVS projects will include a film on gay and lesbian life in the South, a documentary sympathetic to a Black Panther convicted of machine-gunning two New York City policemen, and a film entitled "Trail of Tears: The Ho Chi Minh Trail."

Are these the kind of films you the taxpayer want to pay for? Do they represent the kind of "quality" programming and "alternative" viewing you want to see on your public airwaves? I'll let you decide.

Remember, with public TV and radio, you don't have to tune in, but you still have to pay. Even if you're not watching or listening, it's your tax dollars feeding the meter.

No Taxpayers' Funds

Let me be clear. I am absolutely against using taxpayer funds to set up some kind of conservative network—that would be just as wrong as using public money for liberal cheerleaders.

No doubt about it, public television was a much-needed alternative to the pap that dominated commercial TV in the 1950s and 1960s. But now, seemingly light years later, Americans are living in the middle of a communications revolution. Thanks to satellites, cable TV, fiber optics and videocassettes, viewers and listeners are presented with a staggering array of quality educational and cultural programming and none of it subsidized by you the taxpayer.

Whether it's the Arts & Entertainment Network, the Discovery Channel, Bravo, ESPN, the so-called super stations, CNN, your local video store, and your local library, too, Americans enjoy almost unlimited choice for information and entertainment. Just look at the "Hallmark Hall of Fame" broadcasts on network TV, and you know that there is no such thing as a public TV monopoly on quality entertainment.

It's clear the need for taxpayer-subsidized television is becoming more and more difficult to justify. By the way, despite the claim that your tax dollars and pledges are urgently needed to keep Masterpiece Theater on the air, you should know that Mobil Oil pays the entire tab for that fine show, and also pays PBS stations to air it.

At the very least, America's public broadcasting establishment is in bad need of fine-tuning. But perhaps it's time to change the channel and let the marketplace take control.

If Sesame Street, Masterpiece Theater, Mister Rogers, the Civil War series, or just about any of the "quality" programs on PBS were ever offered on the open market, they would be snapped up quickly by most of the channels mentioned above, and they would flourish—without your tax money.

In these tough economic times—or any time—Congress owes the American taxpayers a thorough review of every dollar we are asked to spend. So stay tuned—the debate over public broadcasting is in the public interest.

"[Public television] is the only place where quality, not profit, counts."

Public Television Already Reflects Mainstream Values

Bruce Christensen and David Britt

Bruce Christensen is president of the Public Broadcasting Service and author of Part I of the following viewpoint. Author of Part II, David Britt, is president and chief executive of the Children's Television Workshop. They contend that public television has been a dramatically successful innovation in American life, producing programs which otherwise would have been unlikely to receive support from a profit-driven market system. They also believe that public television has developed a number of technological innovations, which have furthered the goal of international communication for the good of all.

As you read, consider the following questions:

1. How, according to Christensen, is PBS "our national park of the air"?
2. Why, says Christensen, will the marketplace never eliminate the need for public television?
3. Do Christensen and Britt address the issues of narrow geographical focus or objectionable programming that Dole raised?

Bruce Christensen, "Critical Misperceptions in Senator's View of Public TV," *Kansas City Star*, March 31, 1992. Reprinted with permission. David Britt, "Dole Is Seriously Mistaken About Children's TV Workshop," *Kansas City Star*, March 31, 1992. Reprinted with permission.

I

During the past few weeks, there has been much discussion about public television—some of it on the Senate floor, most of it in the news media. We always welcome the chance to examine our institution—specifically, the resources it provides on and off the screen that make it an essential community educational resource.

Misconceptions About Public Television

Sen. Bob Dole's column (published March 25 [1992] on the Opinion pages of the *Kansas City Star*) includes some misconceptions about public TV that need to be addressed.

First, his notion that the cable boom has eliminated the need for public TV is anachronistic. Few believe it anymore; even fewer mention it. Cable, like its broadcast network counterpart, is designed for profit, pure and simple. It was the Gold Rush of the '80s.

But public TV is a public service. It's our national park of the air. It delivers programming chosen solely on the basis of quality and audience need. And, for nearly 50 years, it has delivered a wide array of exciting and fresh educational services to this nation's elementary and secondary schools and two-thirds of its colleges and universities.

In addition to providing programming and educational services, public TV is a pioneer in communications technology. It was the first national network to distribute programs by satellite; it developed closed captioning for the deaf and descriptive video service for the blind, and piloted a project to link by satellite students and teachers over great distances.

A new satellite, scheduled for launch, will greatly expand the number of channels available for education. Other educational programming providers have been invited to join PBS on the satellite to make access to a wide array of services as easy as possible for teachers.

Anyone who thinks "the marketplace" will bring the best public TV programs to commercial TV is misinformed. Just ask any producer. For example, "The Civil War" producer Ken Burns says of his acclaimed series: "Can you imagine what it would have looked like elsewhere? [Public TV] is the only place on the dial where you can be free of commercials, where you can have a measure of creative control over your project, a lack of interference." In other words, it's the only place where quality, not profit, counts.

And all of the talk about "the marketplace" won't eliminate the need for public service television. When it comes to education, the biggest chain bookstore is no match for the corner public library. Similarly, the local video shop, the commercial TV station and the cable channel are no match for the local public TV station.

Broad Support for Public TV

It is no wonder opinion leaders and "just plain folk" in communities across America volunteer their time and hard-earned money to support their local public TV station. Membership and giving are at an all-time high. Chances are that most of the people reading this newspaper have given to their local public TV station.

Indeed, American taxpayers do have a right to know how their tax dollars for public broadcasting are being spent. Federal appropriations account for 17 percent of public TV money. It funds the best children's programming, news and public affairs programming and documentaries—along with education and technology services—that Americans have come to expect from public television. And yes, I guess you do have to pony up that 17 percent even if you don't watch—annually, it comes out to about $1 per person. It's got to be the best bargain in the federal budget.

Public television is as important today as it was 24 years ago when educational TV stations created the Public Broadcasting Service. Let's keep the discussion going—but stick to the facts.

II

Sen. Robert Dole's statement in the *Star* was filled with misleading and harmful allegations about Children's Television Workshop and "Sesame Street." A few examples:

• Senator Dole suggests that "Sesame Street" gets $14 million in federal funding each year. That's dead wrong. "Sesame Street" has not received any direct federal grants since 1982. Two-thirds of the annual $17 million cost of "Sesame Street" is paid by CTW itself from licensing revenue. The rest is paid by public television stations.

• The $14 million annual taxpayer subsidy Dole complains about actually includes more than $5 million in payments by foreign governments to CTW for the right to bring "Sesame Street" and other CTW educational programs to their children. The federal grants CTW does receive support specific educational programs in math and science. For all the Workshop's educational projects, CTW has leveraged each federal dollar received with more than two dollars of non-governmental support.

• Dole suggests CTW's $58 million endowment fund should bar CTW from receiving federal grants. Such a ban would prohibit federal grants to virtually every educational institution in the country, including the University of Kansas.

• The compensation noted by Dole is not that of either the president or the chief executive officer of CTW. Rather, it is the compensation package of the executive who is responsible for international and domestic product licensing for the Children's Television Workshop. He is instrumental in generating more than $20 million in self-support revenues for "Sesame Street," other educational activities and our endowment. He is not an officer of CTW; he works under contract, negotiated with the advice of outside compensation specialists.

Free Enterprise

The right has its culture—as expressed by television and films and music—all supported by the source considered most appropriate by conservatives: free enterprise. As always serious art—that produced with the intention of expanding aesthetic frontiers or challenging the conventional wisdom—must struggle. It is out of respect for those things which do not fare well in the marketplace—at least not in their own time—that we have chosen to lend the support of government to the arts.

Nicols Fox, *New Art Examiner*, Summer 1989.

The larger portion of his compensation is related to a performance-based incentive program, reviewed and approved by the CTW's Board of Trustees' Personnel & Compensation Committee. This arrangement is not representative of other compensation arrangements at CTW, where this particular executive earns substantially more than the president-chief executive officer and all other staff.

Senator Dole's central suggestion is both misleading and dangerous to the well-being of millions of pre-school children. It is that "Sesame Street" and "Mister Rogers' Neighborhood" should be thrown off public television and placed in the "open market," where they will "flourish." Perhaps he believes commercial broadcasters will broadcast two or three hours of "Sesame Street" each day without any commercial interruption. They can't and won't.

No Commercials

The fact is that no one else—no broadcaster, no cable service—attempts to provide the daily educational service to young children that public television now does—accessible to virtually everyone, without commercial interruption.

This is a mean political season. Notably absent from Dole's recent opinion piece are CTW's contributions to the education of America's children. Nor does he acknowledge the financial contributions—totaling more than $140 million—that we have made from our own revenues to our educational projects. To date, these projects include:

• "Sesame Street," the most popular and effective educational television series ever produced for pre-schoolers, now in its 23rd broadcast season, with 50 million young "graduates" all over the United States.

• "3-2-1 Contact" and "Square One TV," our popular daily series through which millions of American children have gained new understanding of and excitement about the crucial subjects of science and mathematics.

• Our new "Sesame Street" Preschool Educational Project, or "Sesame Street Pep," which is bringing the lessons of the series to the unprecedented numbers of pre-schoolers in child care all over the country to help prepare them for school.

• "Ghostwriter," our new multimedia literacy project which, beginning this fall, will get millions of seven-to-ten-year-olds excited about reading and writing.

When Senator Dole and his colleagues get their "debate" over public television, and if they win it, who will serve the educational needs of America's young children?

"Rock music has become a Trojan Horse, rolling explicit sex and violence into our homes."

Rock Music Should Be Labeled

Tipper Gore

Tipper Gore is co-founder of the Parents' Music Resource Center, an advocacy group that supports record labeling, and has served on the Task Force on Children and Television of the American Academy of Pediatrics. In the mid-1980s, she and her family became concerned about the prevalence of adult language and images in rock music and music videos. In the following viewpoint, she recounts her experiences in that effort. A mother of four, Tipper Gore is married to Vice President Albert Gore.

As you read, consider the following questions:

1. What kinds of music and videos led Gore to found the Parents' Music Resource Center?
2. How, according to Gore, was the labeling proposed "the exact opposite of censorship"?
3. How was record labeling a compromise between prohibition and total freedom?

From *Raising PG Kids in an X-Rated Society* by Tipper Gore. Copyright © 1987 by Mary Elizabeth Gore. Excerpted by permission of the publisher, Abingdon Press.

I became aware of the emergence of explicit and violent images in the world of music through my children. In December 1984, I purchased Prince's best-selling album *Purple Rain* for my eleven-year-old daughter. I had seen Prince on the cover of magazines, and I knew that he was the biggest pop idol in years. My daughter wanted his album because she had heard the single "Let's Go Crazy" on the radio. But when we brought the album home, put it on our stereo, and listened to it together, we heard the words to another song, "Darling Nikki": "I knew a girl named Nikki/Guess [you] could say she was a sex fiend/I met her in a hotel lobby/Masturbating with a magazine." The song went on and on, in a similar manner. I couldn't believe my ears! The vulgar lyrics embarrassed both of us. At first, I was stunned—then I got mad! Millions of Americans were buying *Purple Rain* with no idea what to expect. Thousands of parents were giving the album to their children—many even younger than my daughter.

"Mature" Themes

Around that time, my two younger daughters, ages six and eight, began asking me about things they had seen on MTV, the music video channel on cable television. I had always thought that videos had great potential as a dramatic new art form, but I had not watched many. I began watching more often, and I observed that several included adult (or at least "mature") themes and images. "Mom, why is the teacher taking off her clothes?" my six-year-old asked, after watching Van Halen's *Hot for Teacher*, in which a "teacher" does a striptease act for the boys in her class.

I sat down with my kids and watched videos like Motley Crüe's *Looks That Kill*, with scantily clad women being captured and imprisoned in cages by a studded-leather-clad male band. In *Photograph*, by Def Leppard, we saw a dead woman tied up with barbed wire. The Scorpions' *Rock You Like a Hurricane* showed a man tied to the walls of a torture chamber and a singer being choked by a woman. These images frightened my children; they frightened *me*! The graphic sex and the violence were too much for us to handle.

Other parents were experiencing the same rude awakening. One day in early 1985, my friend Susan Baker came by to talk about her concerns. Susan and her husband, U.S. Treasury Secretary James Baker, have eight children. She told me that two of her friends were getting ready to take action on the issue of pornographic and violent images in music, and asked if I would be interested in signing a letter inviting others to a meeting to hear more about the excesses in some rock music.

I was so angry about the songs my children and I had heard

that I quickly agreed to join Susan Baker in doing something about it. Susan was working with Sally Nevius, a former dean of admissions at Mount Vernon College in Washington. Sally and her husband, the former chairman of the District of Columbia City Council, had an eleven-year-old daughter. Also assisting Susan Baker was Pam Howar, a businesswoman with a seven-year-old daughter.

Ramirez/Copley News Service. Reprinted with permission.

We decided to establish the nonprofit Parents' Music Resource Center, to be known as the PMRC. In May of 1985, we set out to alert other parents in our community. Sally arranged for Jeff Ling, a former rock musician who is now a youth minister at a suburban Virginia church, to give a slide presentation graphically illustrating the worst excesses in rock music, from lyrics to concert performances to rock magazines aimed at the teenage market. We invited the public, community leaders, our friends (some of whom hold public office), and representatives of the music industry. Our hope was to generate a discussion of the issue, raise public awareness, and begin a dialogue with people in the industry. To our surprise, more than 350 people showed up at our first meeting on May 15, 1985, at St. Columba's Church in Washington, D.C.

To my knowledge, no music industry representatives attended

this meeting, with one very important exception: Eddie Fritts, president of the National Association of Broadcasters (NAB), unable to attend himself, had sent his wife, Martha Dale Fritts, and two NAB staff members. They brought with them a letter that Mr. Fritts had just written and sent to eight hundred group station owners, which alerted them to growing concern among the public over "porn rock":

> The lyrics of some recent rock records and the tone of their related music videos are fast becoming a matter of public debate. The subject has drawn national attention through articles in publications like *Newsweek* and *USA Today* and feature reports on TV programs like "Good Morning, America."

> Many state that they are extremely troubled by the sexually explicit and violent language of some of today's songs. . . .

> The pre-teen and teen audiences are heavy listeners, viewers and buyers of rock music. In some communities, like Washington, D.C., parents and other interested citizens are organizing to see what they can do about the music in question, which at least one writer has dubbed "porn rock."

> I wanted you, as one of the leaders in the broadcasting industry, to be aware of this situation. . . .

> It is, of course, up to each broadcast licensee to make its own decisions as to the manner in which it carries out its programming responsibilities under the Communications Act.

Two weeks later, Mr. Fritts wrote to the heads of forty-five major record companies:

> At its May meeting, NAB's Executive Committee asked that I write you to request that all recordings made available to broadcasters in the future be accompanied by copies of the songs' lyrics. It appears that providing this material to broadcasters would place very little burden on the recording industry, while greatly assisting the decision making of broadcast management and programming staffs. . . .

Considering the initial NAB response, we were off to a good start, but what should we do next? How could we make ourselves heard by the giants of the record industry, like Warner Brothers, Capitol, and RCA?

A Secret Ally

By happy chance, we gained an ally in the recording industry who could help us find our way through the music business. Throughout the ensuing campaign, he gave us invaluable advice—on the condition that he never be identified.

Our secret ally held an important position in the record industry. Like us, he was sickened and disgusted by the trend toward pornography and violence in some rock music. He advised us to set up a meeting with Stan Gortikov at the Recording Industry

Association of America (RIAA), the trade group that represents all major record companies. Gortikov had been president of the RIAA since 1972, and before that he had headed Capitol Records. He agreed to meet with us in early June.

Our strategy was simple. We felt it was crucial to publicize the excesses in song lyrics and videos, the source of our concern. We were convinced that most parents are either unaware of the trends in rock music, or uncertain what to do about them. We decided to get the word out and build a consumer movement to put pressure on the industry. From the start, we recognized that the only solution would involve some voluntary action on the part of the industry. We wanted industry leaders to assume direct corporate responsibility for their products. The problem was to persuade an industry profiting from excesses to exercise some self-restraint.

In 1984, the National Congress of Parents and Teachers (the National PTA) had called on record companies to label their products for sexual content, violence, and profanity, in order to inform parents about inappropriate materials. The PTA had written to thirty-two record companies but had only received three responses. And those refused to discuss the issue further. Our ally advised us not to deal with the companies on an individual basis.

He suggested that we present our plans to the RIAA's Gortikov and not leave him any choice. Our source said the best way to catch the industry's attention was on the airwaves. So the PMRC launched a grass-roots media campaign that soon took on a life of its own.

From News Story to National Issue

From June to November 1985, we held dozens of meetings, participated in frequent conference calls, and exchanged numerous letters, as we sought solutions palatable to the industry and to the National PTA and the PMRC. As our negotiations intensified, the issue quickly became a national one. . . .

The media campaign took care of itself. A small story about our first public meeting appeared in the "Style" section of the *Washington Post*. Before we knew it, we were besieged with requests for interviews. Kandy Stroud, a journalist, musician, and mother of three, had earlier written a "My Turn" column entitled "Stop Pornographic Rock" for the May 6, 1985, edition of *Newsweek*. She immediately received an invitation to appear on "Good Morning, America." Kandy and Pam Howar appeared on "Panorama," a Washington television show. Soon after that, I did an hour-long radio talk show in Oklahoma City, and Susan Baker and Sally Nevius participated in a similar show in another state. . . .

The PMRC proposed a unique mechanism to increase consumer choice in the marketplace instead of limiting it. Our approach was the direct opposite of censorship. We called for more information, not less. We did not advocate a ban of even the most offensive albums or tapes. We simply urged that the consumer be forewarned through the use of warning labels and/or printed lyrics visible on the outside packaging of music products. Critics used the smokescreen of censorship to dodge the real issue, which was lack of any corporate responsibility for the impact their products may have on young people.

The PMRC sought to balance the precious right of artistic free speech with the right of parents to protect their children from explicit messages that they are not mature enough to understand or deal with. These two rights are not mutually exclusive and one should not be sacrificed for the other. Records, tapes, and videos are consumer products, mass-produced, distributed, and marketed to the public. Children and parents of children constitute the bulk of that consuming public.

Don't Accept the Message

The popular culture is worth paying attention to. It is the air we breathe, and 2 Live Crew is a pesky new pollutant. The opinion industry's advice is generally to buy a gas mask or stop breathing. ("If you don't like their album, don't buy it," one such genius wrote.) But by monitoring, complaining, boycotting, we might actually get the 2 Live Pollutants out of our air. Why should our daughters have to grow up in a culture in which musical advice on the domination and abuse of women is accepted as entertainment?

John Leo, *U.S. News & World Report*, July 2, 1990.

The PMRC and the National PTA have agreed that these musical products should enjoy all the rights and privileges guaranteed by the First Amendment. But as Thomas Jefferson once said, when excesses occur, the best guarantee of free speech is *more* speech, not less. That's all we asked for—awareness and disclosure. Our proposal amounted to nothing more than truth-in-packaging, a time-honored principle in our free-enterprise system.

In this information age, such consumer information gives parents an important tool for making choices for their children. Without it, parental guidance in the matter of available entertainment is virtually impossible. The PMRC proposal does *not* infringe on the First Amendment. It does *not* raise a constitutional issue. But it *does* seek to reform marketing practices by asking for better and more informative packaging. And it *does* seek to inform consumers when artistic expression borders on what legendary singer Smokey Robinson has called "musical pornography."

Who decides which songs are musical pornography? Only the record company can make that decision—not the government, as some would have us believe, and not an outside censorship board, as others have charged. The music industry, which allowed these excesses to develop, would be asked to take responsibility for the product it markets to the public.

In fact, we are talking about products primarily written for children, marketed to children, and sold to children. In this country we rightly treat children differently from adults; most people feel that children should not enjoy the same access to adult material as adults. Children are not allowed into R-rated movies if they are under seventeen. In most places, minors are not allowed to buy *Playboy* and *Penthouse* or go into adult bookstores.

If no one under eighteen can buy *Penthouse* magazine, why should children be subjected to explicit album covers and lyrics that are even worse? If we have decided it is not in the best interest of society to allow children into X-rated bookstores, why should they be subjected to hard-core porn in the local record shop? A recent album from the Dead Kennedys band contained a graphic poster of multiple erect penises penetrating vaginas. Where's the difference?

In the hands of a few warped artists, their brand of rock music has become a Trojan Horse, rolling explicit sex and violence into our homes. This ruse made us gasp at the cynicism of the recording company executives who control the music business. They found it easy to confuse the issue by throwing out cries of censorship while refusing to address the real problem. They dodged the real point—that in a free society we can affirm the First Amendment and also protect the rights of children and adults who seek to avoid the twisted tyranny of explicitness in the public domain.

Proposing Alternatives to the Music Industry

At a second meeting with the RIAA's Stan Gortikov, on May 31, 1985, we presented a letter to him signed by sixteen wives of United States representatives and senators:

> It is our concern that some of the music which the recording industry sells today increasingly portrays explicit sex and violence, and glorifies the use of drugs and alcohol. It is indiscriminately available to persons of any age through record stores and the media.

> These messages reach young children and early teenagers at a crucial age when they are developing lifelong value systems.

191

Their minds are often not yet discerning enough to reject the destructive influences and anti-social behaviour engendered by what they hear and see in these products.

Because of the excesses that exist in the music industry today, we petition the industry to exercise voluntary self-restraint perhaps by developing guidelines and/or a rating system, such as that of the movie industry, for use by parents in order to protect our younger children from such mature themes.

Braced with this letter, Mr. Gortikov pledged to work swiftly within the music industry.

Over the next few months, we negotiated several alternatives with the RIAA. We began by asking for a categorical rating system based on content, then suggested using the symbol "R" to designate explicit albums. Finally, we joined forces with the National PTA and its 5.8 million members. Together with the RIAA we called for a consumer warning label on explicit or violent albums or for full disclosure of lyrics. "We recommend this course of action because we believe it protects consumers by providing them with valuable information while respecting recording artists' First Amendment rights," said National PTA president Ann Kahn.

Pam Howar of the PMRC urged the industry to "create a uniform standard to be used to define what constitutes blatant, explicit lyric content." We thought the ideal solution would be a label (or some symbol) to advise the consumer about explicit lyrics in a particular album. Printed lyrics would also enable the consumer to make an informed decision appropriate for their child's age. Since most albums would not concern parents, there had to be some way to flag those that might. . . .

A Uniform Standard

While we were calling publicly for consumer warning labels on albums containing explicit lyrics, and for an industry panel to set guidelines defining explicit material, we worked feverishly behind the scenes to obtain industry endorsement of a uniform standard—one written by the industry itself, not by us. The standard would loosely define what constituted blatantly explicit lyric content. Meanwhile, the Musical Majority and others lined up pop stars to blast "music censorship" and the women who would "ban rock and roll." Our ally in the industry had warned us that we would be no match for prominent artists calling us "censoring prudes" or worse, as industry leaders fought to protect the status quo and their economic interests.

By this time, the United States Congress had begun to take an interest in the issue, and many members considered holding hearings. In September 1985, Senator John Danforth of Missouri scheduled a hearing before the Senate's commerce committee, which he chaired. The commerce committee has jurisdiction over communications issues, and wanted to investigate the prevalence of pornographic, violent rock lyrics for its own information—not to consider any legislation. . . .

The September 19 hearing certainly brought the issue out for public debate. It turned out to be the most widely publicized media event in congressional history. A seat in the hearing room was the hottest ticket in town all year.

Both sides turned out in force. Susan Baker and I testified for the PMRC, and Jeff Ling gave his slide show. The National PTA also sent representatives who testified. Frank Zappa, John Denver, and Dee Snider of Twisted Sister also appeared.

The hearing did not seek to reach any consensus, but on the whole we were pleased to see the facts come out. Twisted Sister's Dee Snider told the committee that he was a Christian who did not smoke, drink, or do drugs, and insisted that he had been unfairly accused. A member of the committee—my husband—asked him the full name of his fan club, SMF Fans of Twisted Sister. Replied Snider, "It stands for Sick Mother Fucking Fans of Twisted Sister."

Agreement with the RIAA

After the Senate hearing, the negotiations produced results that all parties felt represented a workable and fair arrangement. We decided to make a major compromise—to accept the formation of an RIAA policy statement on explicit lyrics, and drop our request for a uniform standard of what is or is not explicit. We would also drop our request for an R rating on albums or tapes to designate explicit products, in exchange for the warning "Explicit Lyrics—Parental Advisory." We agreed to give the compromise a chance to work in the marketplace, and to monitor it jointly and assess its effectiveness a year later. We also agreed to cease the media campaign for one year. On November 1, 1985, the RIAA, the National PTA, and the PMRC jointly announced the agreement at the National Press Club in Washington.

"Record labels have targeted primarily heavy metal and rap music, the two most politically uncompromising forms of commercial art in America reaching the broadest base, working-class audience perhaps ever reached by any art form."

Labeling Rock Music Leads to Repression

Danny Alexander

Long active in music reviewing and anti-censorship campaigns, Danny Alexander, in the following viewpoint, discusses the controversy surrounding rock, rap, and social violence. Alexander contends that labeling of music is not a simple, reasonable approach to social responsibility, but instead has led to exclusion of music from record stores and the airwaves. In some places, he says, rappers, hard rock fans and disc jockeys have been arrested, fined, and otherwise harassed, producing a general atmosphere of tension and intimidation in America.

As you read, consider the following questions:

1. How, according to Alexander, does the labeling campaign provide a basis for censorship and harassment of fans?
2. What does the author believe is the real agenda of the anti-rock and anti-rap forces?
3. How, according to Alexander, does record labeling affect artists, store owners, and audiences? Why, in his view, is this impact most severe on audiences?

Danny Alexander, *Targeting the Street: The Truth About Record Labels*, a monograph written explicitly for inclusion in the present volume.

It all seemed innocent enough at the beginning—if not even naïve. In her May 6, 1985, "My Turn" column for *Newsweek*, Parents Music Resource Center (PMRC) journalist Kandy Stroud laid out the agenda to curb the rising tide of "tasteless, graphic and gratuitously sexual songs" in today's rock music.

She made her point somewhat persuasively, starting with references to masturbation and sexual intercourse in Prince and Madonna songs and then padding her illustrations with violently sexual scenes culled from heavy metal albums.

She closed with a call to action that revealed her real motivation and purpose:

> Legislative action may be needed, or better yet, a measure of self-restraint. If distillers can voluntarily keep their products off the public airwaves, then the record industry can also curb porn rock—or, at the very least, make sure that kids under 17 are not allowed into sexually explicit concerts.

> And what about the musicians themselves? If forty-six pop superstars can cooperate to raise millions of dollars for African famine relief with their hit "We Are the World," why can't musicians also ensure that America's own youth will be fed a diet of rock music that is not only good to dance to but healthy for their hearts and minds and souls as well?

In an effort to steer popular music in this healthy direction, Stroud proposed that the record industry self-censor itself with a system of "voluntary" record labeling. The end result of this campaign is that today, most major labels print a sticker that says "Parental Advisory Explicit Lyrics," to let parents know which albums to buy for their children and which to avoid. Proponents of labeling argue that this system is no different than ingredient labels on food, or the labeling system that is used for movies.

They are wrong. For starters, stigmatizing a record because of a word someone may deem explicit (a particularly ridiculous example being the word "pee" on Prince's 68-minute *Graffiti Bridge* album) without also discussing the musicianship, the context for the word choice or the themes that dominate the record (in this example faith and renewal) could hardly be called an accurate listing of ingredients.

Parental Advisory

I'll never forget standing in a record store when a mother held up a copy of rap group Boogie Down Productions' *Edutainment* and asked why it had a sticker. The sales clerk said it probably had some curse words on it. The woman said, "Oh, well I don't want that!" She promptly slammed one of the most uplifting, sophisticated expositions on Afrocentricity and contemporary society ever recorded back into its slot, mentally lumping this record in with the likes of 2 Live Crew. So much for parental advisory.

What is most disturbing about record labeling are the ways in which it seems to serve as a means to more generally (as Kandy Stroud put it in her manifesto) "curb" rock, particularly heavy metal and rap music.

Banning Rock

Major music distributors have made it clear that they will not carry albums that bear warning stickers. Musicians who produce albums that do not fit the arbitrary criteria set by local censors will be shut out of the distribution system. Major labels won't release albums that they think might not be sold in major outlets. Independent labels are already hard-pressed to find store owners willing to stock their products.

No More Censorship Defense Fund, *Fact Sheet #4.*

Since the September 1985 Senate Committee on Commerce, Science, and Transportation meetings led by Missouri senator John Danforth and [former] Tennessee senator Al Gore (whose wife, along with Secretary of State James Baker's wife created the Parents Music Resource Center) record labeling has been mandated through a series of threatening legislative gestures and cowering responses by the record industry.

It's understandable to see why the record industry cowered. In September 1986, the PMRC's "First Annual Pig-Pickin'" fundraiser in Poolesville, Maryland, featured a cast of heavy-weights and was bankrolled by a heap of money. The summit-disguised-as-picnic cost $75 for general admission, $200 for a patron and $1500 per corporation. Attendees included Senator Lloyd Bentsen, the Bakers, the Gores, the Danforths, key Barry Goldwater and Bush/Reagan advisor Dean Burch, White House advisor and CEO of The Magazine Publishers Association William Gorog, former Nixon aide and Marriot v.p. Fred Malek and Reagan tax advisor Bruce Thompson.

Proposed Legislation

Allegedly after meeting Tipper Gore at an Eagle Forum presentation, Missouri representative Jean Dixon drafted a bill mandating warning labels for records in 1989. By 1990, thirteen states had drafted similar bills. At an April 5, 1990 press conference, the PMRC, the PTA, and NARM (the National Association of Record Merchandisers) announced that those thirteen states (along with five others considering such legislation) would withdraw their bills if the industry adopted a more rigid "voluntary" labeling system. For the PMRC, this was the best of all possible solutions: though such laws might be found unconstitutional (after all, they certainly could be shown to abridge free speech), without even one law being passed, the desired mechanism for control had been achieved.

Why all this interest in controlling rock music? Probably not because teenagers might masturbate in front of their stereos. Since their origins, record labels have targeted primarily heavy metal and rap music, the two most politically uncompromising forms of commercial art in America reaching the broadest base, working-class audience perhaps ever reached by any art form. In a country that is on the brink of economic collapse (which has been apparent to anyone paying attention for at least a decade, certainly by Black Monday in 1987), it is not surprising that many equate a record like Ice-T's "Cop Killer" with yelling "fire" in a crowded theater, and that's the way such controversial music is being treated.

Censorship, the L.A. Riots, and Record Labels

The aftermath of the Los Angeles riots presents a particularly telling series of events which, even if they share no direct causal relationship, suggest a new tolerance for censorship on a local and national level.

Ironically, considering the popular response, the California State Assembly's Special Committee on the Los Angeles Crisis stated, "poverty, segregation, lack of education and employment opportunities, wide-spread perceptions of police abuse and unequal consumer services [are] the principal grievances which led to the civil disturbances of the 1960s. Little has changed in 1992 Los Angeles." But our top political leaders quickly found a means to blame the victim, or those who speak for the victims of such abject poverty.

Newsweek, New York Newsday, and the *Washington Post* all wrote articles tying rap music (probably not Sister Souljah, but Public Enemy?) to the rebellion. As the riots flared, Barstow, California (between Los Angeles and Las Vegas), attempted to prohibit the sale of rap music to minors. After the riots, library officials in Lynnwood, Washington, ordered the rap group N.W.A. removed from their shelves. Time Warner's board of directors formed an editorial committee to censor books, records, and videos, one committee member pushing for the elimination of all products that criticize the police. The Shreveport, Louisiana, Department of Parks and Recreation cancelled an afternoon concert by thrash and rap acts because a flier promoting the event advocated free speech.

In August, after more than a month of attacks from organized police groups, Congress, and George Bush, and after duplicitous signals from Time Warner, Ice-T decided to remove "Cop Killer" from its *Body Count* album. A few months later, Ice-T was dropped from the label altogether. In the wake of the controversy, the Tommy Boy label dropped Almighty RSO and Live Squad for attacking police brutality and refused to put out rapper Paris's album because of the song, "Bush Killa." Warner refused to distribute Kool G Rap's album, while rappers Intelligent Hoodlum, Boo-Yaa Tribe, and Da Lench Mob all had to remove controversial songs from their albums. On top of all these individual attacks, despite its popularity, mainstream radio plays almost no rap anymore, which prompted one of the most famous rappers, Ice Cube, to stage a pirate radio broadcast to debut his album in response to the Los Angeles rebellion.

Corporate Censorship

Corporate censorship of the marketplace is driving even mainstream rap artists underground. Labels are refusing to produce controversial rap, distributors won't handle it and the airwaves won't broadcast it. The lesson that seems to have been learned from the LA rebellion is, if this art form can sensitize the American people to a volatile situation, rather than encourage open discussion and possible revolution, we better shut it down.

In that sense, today's censorship tends to take the shape of a class war—not necessarily against the artists, but certainly against the fans who find it harder and harder to hear their favorite music, that which speaks of their anger, hopes and fears. Racist anxieties and other bourgeois family values are being used as a means for determining what music is suitable for public consumption. One of the most powerful censorship organizations in the country, Focus on the Family, which features PMRC founder Susan Baker on its board of directors, publishes a monthly magazine that blacklists music that is anti-family. This year's targets included not only the rap group Naughty by Nature, but also country singer Reba McEntire (for "distrust of men") and metal band Mötley Crüe. The common denominator being that the majority of all these artists' fans are working class—in this day and age, with little hope of a future.

In fact, young hard rock fans have it almost as bad as rap fans. Touring behind its 1989 album *And Justice For All*, the politically confrontational Metallica faced concert cancellations and poor promotion in one city after another because of smear campaigns that painted the group as satanists who promote suicide (wrong on both counts). About the time of the Los Angeles rebellion, a teen in Fort Smith, Arkansas, was arrested for wearing a Van Halen *For Unlawful Carnal Knowledge* t-shirt (because of the acronym), and rock shows by GWAR and Pearl Jam were stopped in Athens, Georgia, and Seattle, Washington, respectively.

What do the majority of the above-named artists have in common? Labeled albums. All of the big censorship cases—the 2 Live Crew arrests, the sting operation on 9 record stores in Nebraska, the arrests of record retailers in Alexander City, Alabama—revolve around the distribution of labeled material. After following the trend since its origins with his newsletter *Rock & Rap Confidential*, rock writer Dave Marsh states, "Labels are catastrophic. Labeling is an implicit guilty plea. It's not a protection—it's a target. Ask Time Warner if labeling Ice-T's record protected them. If they put a label on your record, you're going to get prosecuted. And you won't be tried by the sophisticated laws of Silicon Valley—you're going to be tried under the laws of the Bible Belt."

And if the artist isn't destroyed, someone in the way probably will be. Any retailer familiar with Florida record store owner Charles Freeman's case knows that, while 2 Live Crew had the money and the publicity to win its case, Freeman was still convicted of selling the album, lost his business and went to jail—for selling a *labeled* record to an adult!

The First Amendment works best if you have plenty of cash to fight your cases, and the small record store owners who stand up against censorship are those most vulnerable to financial ruin. As for alternatives, most chain stores don't carry labeled records at all. Retailers are running scared, and the First Amendment doesn't reach down to affect the actions of those in private business. Given a choice between going to court or censoring merchandise, labels and distributors are taking the logical way out. One 2 Live Crew victory doesn't make up for the message sent to small store owners and the thousands of other acts who are never signed and go unheard because of the resultant chilling effect.

Kandy Stroud may not have known what she was starting, but you can bet the VIPs at the Pig Pickin' Summit did. Looking back at the Quayle and Clinton responses to the riots, I can't help but admire the savvy of the then governor of Arkansas (who made it clear on MTV, along with his running mate, he was pro-labeling). After all, if you want to put down a rebellion, you don't take aim at a dry sitcom about an uptight, upper-middle-class white anchorwoman. You aim for the street.

Periodical Bibliography

The following articles have been selected to supplement the diverse views presented in this chapter.

Art News	"Obscenity: What the Supreme Court Says," October 1989.
Jeff Bounds	"Heavy Meddle," *Mother Jones*, January 1990.
Robert Brustein	"The First Amendment and the N.E.A.," *The New Republic*, September 11, 1989.
Christianity Today	"Pornography Foes Urge Increased Awareness," April 14, 1990.
Arthur Danto	"Art and Taxpayers," *The Nation*, August 21/28, 1989.
Bill Dedman	"Bible Belt Blowhard," *Mother Jones*, November/December 1992.
Ted Guest	"The Drive to Make America Porn-Free," *U.S. News & World Report*, February 6, 1989.
Timothy Healey	"Government—A Good Patron but Bad Censor," *The New York Times*, September 15, 1989.
Robert Hughes	"A Loony Parody of Cultural Democracy," *Time*, August 14, 1989.
Henry Hyde	"The Culture War," *National Review*, April 30, 1990.
Carol Iannone	"From 'Lolita' to 'Piss Christ,'" *Commentary*, January 1990.
Hilton Kramer	"Is Art Above the Laws of Decency?" *The New York Times*, July 2, 1989.
John Leo	"Rock 'n' Roll's Hatemongering," *U.S. News & World Report*, March 19, 1990.
Dave Marsh	"Wanted for Attitude: The Right-Wing Attack on Rock," *Village Voice*, October 10, 1989.
Tom Matthews	"Fine Art or Foul?" *Newsweek*, July 2, 1990.
Stephan Salisbury	"Wild in the Streets: Sex, Cities, and the NEA," *American Poetry Review*, November/December 1992.
Jennifer Steinhauer	"Prosecute Porn? It's on the Decline," *The Wall Street Journal*, December 28, 1989.
Sandy Tolan	"Dial 1-800-Censor," *The New York Times*, May 7, 1993.
U.S. News & World Report	"Should Dirty Lyrics Be Against the Law?" June 25, 1990.
Richard Woodbury	"A Smut Buster Battles Sin in the City," *Time*, May 29, 1989.

For Further Discussion

Chapter 1

1. Bloom contends that students today do not read, or like to read. Yet Reed suggests that the problem is that their assigned reading does not relate to their own experience. Who is more persuasive?

2. Barton argues that a number of legal opinions support his view that America is a Christian nation. What types of opinions are these, and when were they issued? Do they contradict current legal rulings by the United States Supreme Court?

3. Boston concentrates on present-day Supreme Court rulings on matters of church-state relations. Why does he emphasize the difference between these and those that formerly prevailed? Has American society evolved a better, or a worse view of these relations?

4. Puritans undoubtedly contributed much to the American character. Do we still need their virtues today, or are they outmoded and irrelevant? Find evidence in the viewpoints to support your opinion.

5. Parrington takes a dim view of Puritanism; does he allow the force of his hostility to cloud his judgment? Is he fair to the Puritan tradition?

6. Auster believes that our American identity is threatened by immigration; how is present-day immigration different from that in the past? Are Alexander Hamilton's views on national identity still viable after two hundred years?

7. After reading all the viewpoints in this chapter, how many cultures do you think we have in America? Or, how many cultural traditions? Should we try to have only one culture, or be content with many?

8. What is meant by the term "world culture"? Is this a reality, or only a possibility? What advantages, or disadvantages, would such a culture have?

Chapter 2

1. Adler defends his basis for selecting the Great Books, but what is that basis? What criteria would you use if you were

assuming that responsibility? What is Gitlin's basis for developing a curriculum?

2. What, in D'Souza's view, are the connections between left-wing rhetoric in the 1950s, and that of the "politically correct" movement of today? What does his antagonism against the left tell you about his own political views?

3. Williams believes that certain just gains should be defended in contemporary collegiate life. What are those gains? Are they really threatened by anyone, or is the threat mostly in her imagination?

4. What is meant by the term "multiculturalism"? Does it have different meanings for different people? Is one culture "better" than another? If so, how would you decide?

Chapter 3

1. On what basis does Bloom prefer classical to rock music? How do we decide which music is "better"? Do you agree with him that rock music promotes adolescent attitudes and life patterns too far into adult life, so that young people don't properly mature?

2. Why do you think that Madonna is so controversial? Is it because she is independent and free in spirit? Or is it because she restricts her artistic expression as a woman to sexual roles, often of a deviant (sadomasochistic) nature?

3. What is the content of rap music, according to Teachout? What is its content according to George? How do you think that we decide the social value of music?

Chapter 4

1. Why was the National Endowment for the Arts created? Has it been true to its original vision, or has it been corrupted, as some say, like everything else in Washington?

2. What, according to the various authors in this chapter, should be the role of the government in the arts? How does the government decide which art should be supported?

3. Dole believes that public television should reflect mainstream values. What are those values for him? For Rohrabacher? For Danforth? How do we decide what is "mainstream"?

4. Gore believes that she and others in the effort to label rock music have been moderate and willing to compromise. What was the nature of this compromise? Does such a compromise have the force of law?

5. Alexander contends that labeling has led to repression. What evidence does he cite for this view? Have you experienced anything similar in your own life?

General

1. For much of our history, America has been notably optimistic in both philosophy and culture. More recently, however, there has been, at least for some, a certain shift toward pessimism. Is this a real shift in American society? If so, why has it occurred?

2. Many of the debates on culture revolve around defining acceptable standards for art that may be considered obscene, pornographic, or otherwise unacceptable. How do you think we should define what is acceptable? Who do you think should decide what is acceptable under the law?

3. The First Amendment to the Constitution says that Congress shall make no law abridging freedom of speech or the press. Should we have limits on these freedoms? If so, what should they be? How do we constitutionally provide for both freedom and responsibility?

4. Some writers view multiculturalism as a threat to America's national identity. What are their reasons for this view? Do you agree with them? Why or why not?

5. Do you think that art merely reflects underlying trends in our society, or does it lead those trends?

6. Do you think American society and culture will be able to solve our problems? Are we capable of having a culture worthy of the American dream? Why or why not?

Organizations to Contact

The editors have compiled the following list of organizations that are concerned with the issues debated in this book. All have publications or information available for interested readers. For best results, allow as much time as possible for the organizations to respond. The descriptions below are derived from materials provided by the organizations. This list was compiled at the date of publication. Names, addresses, and phone numbers of organizations are subject to change.

Accuracy in Media (AIM)
1275 K St. NW, Suite 1150
Washington, DC 20005
(202) 371-6710

AIM is a conservative group that investigates claims of factual errors in the media, and regularly requests that such errors be corrected. They issue a bimonthly *AIM Report*.

African Americans for Humanism (AAH)
Box 664
Buffalo, NY 14226-0664
(716) 636-7571

The AAH is dedicated to developing humanism in the African-American community, and exists for those who are unchurched or free from religion and who are looking for a rational and ethical approach to life. It is especially concerned with fighting racism through humanistic education, and publishes a quarterly newsletter.

American Civil Liberties Union (ACLU)
132 W. 43rd St.
New York, NY 10036
(212) 944-9800

The ACLU is one of the oldest civil liberties organizations, and is committed to the defense of the First Amendment and other constitutional rights such as due process and equal protection of the law. It is active in most cities and university communities, and issues a monthly, *Civil Liberties Alert*.

American Conservative Union (ACU)
38 Ivy St. SE
Washington, DC 20003
(202) 546-6555

The ACU concentrates on anti-communism, the free market system and other conservative issues. It supplies speakers on these issues, and publishes *New Freedom*, a quarterly.

American Family Association
PO Drawer 2440
Tupelo, MS 38803-9988
(601) 844-5036

The association has concentrated its activities against obscenity in museums, movies, the National Endowment for the Arts, and network television, using newspaper ads, petitions, consumer boycotts, and so on, organized via direct mail.

Americans United for Separation of Church and State
8120 Fenton St.
Silver Spring, MD 20910-4781
(301) 589-3707

This organization was founded in 1947 and works to preserve the constitutional guarantee of separation of church and state. It publicizes information on current aspects of this issue, including violations of the law and pending legislation in *Church and State*, a monthly journal.

Christian Coalition
Box 1990
Chesapeake, VA 23327
(804) 424-2630

The coalition, formed in 1989, aims to make government more responsive to the concerns of evangelical Christians and pro-family Catholics. It further seeks to reverse moral decay in America by training Christians for effective political action, through issuing scorecards on Congress, voter registration campaigns, etc. The coalition publishes a newspaper, *Christian American*, six times per year.

Eagle Forum
Box 618
Alton, IL 62002
(618) 462-5415

The forum has been active in pro-family traditional values and patriotic causes, as well as opposition to abortion rights and other feminist issues. It publishes a monthly newsletter, the *Phyllis Schlafly Report*.

Fairness and Accuracy in Reporting (FAIR)
130 West 25th St.
New York, NY 10001
(212) 633-6700

FAIR investigates conservative bias in news coverage, and issues *Extra!*, a newsletter that is a source of current information on this type of censorship.

Freedom from Religion Foundation
Box 750
Madison, WI 53701
(608) 256-8900

The foundation is committed to grassroots activism in defense of secular humanism and atheism, and has participated in lawsuits in defense of separation of church and state. It sponsors student essay contests, annual conventions, and publicizes current events in *Freethought Today*, a monthly newspaper.

The Heritage Foundation
214 Massachusetts Ave. NE
Washington, DC 20002
(202) 546-4400

The foundation conducts research, promotes seminars and conferences, and issues a range of publications in support of free enterprise and limited government. It played a major role in outlining political options for the Reagan administration.

Institute for First Amendment Studies
Box 589
Great Barrington, VT 01230
(413) 274-3786

The institute closely monitors operations of the Christian Coalition and similar conservative organizations on issues of freedom of speech and press. It issues a monthly newsletter, *The Freedom Writer*.

The Literary Network
154 Christopher St., Suite 3C
New York, NY 10014
(212) 741-9110

The network concentrates on legislative and government agency monitoring, on behalf of writers, and advocates grassroots contacts with Congress to protect First Amendment rights.

National Coalition Against Censorship
275 7th Ave.
New York, NY 10001
(212) 807-6222

The coalition represents more than forty national organizations involved with action against suppression of free speech and press. They issue newsletters and pamphlets.

National Coalition Against Pornography
800 Compton Rd.
Cincinnati, OH 45231-9964
(513) 521-6227

This organization links pornography to violence, and supports local legislation to eliminate or regulate adult bookstores, cinemas, etc. They have issued a number of books and other publications.

Parents' Music Resource Center
1500 Arlington Blvd., Suite 300
Arlington, VA 22209
(703) 527-9466

The center was established in 1984 to review the content of records and videos for obscene or pornographic content, and has been active in the effort to secure agreements with companies to label records for offensive lyrics.

People for the American Way (PAW)
2000 M St. NW, Suite 400
Washington, DC 20036
(202) 467-4999

PAW began from a base in the media, and has expanded to include religious, business, and community leaders committed to organizing for the defense of toleration and liberal principles. It monitors right-wing activity and issues periodic reports on this subject.

Teachers for a Democratic Culture (TDC)
Box 6405
Evanston, IL 60204
(312) 743-3662

TDC consists of college and university faculty who are committed to principles of diversity and multiculturalism in the curricula and other activities of these institutions. They have sponsored conferences, and issue a regular newsletter.

Bibliography of Books

Patricia Aufderheide, ed.
: *Beyond P.C.: Toward a Politics of Understanding.* St. Paul: Graywolf Press, 1992. An anthology of documents from both sides of the "P.C." debate.

David H. Bennett
: *The Party of Fear.* New York: Vintage, 1990. A narrative history of anti-foreign political movements in America, from the Know-Nothings to the New Right.

William J. Bennett
: *The Devaluing of America: The Fight for Our Culture and Our Children.* New York: Summit, 1992. A former secretary of education and chairman of the National Endowment for the Humanities gives a personal account of the making and unmaking of education, drug control, and cultural policy.

Paul Berman, ed.
: *Debating P.C.: The Controversy over Political Correctness on College Campuses.* New York: Dell, 1992. A selection of essays on "P.C.," the canon, free speech, and public schools.

Sidney Blumenthal
: *The Rise of the Counter-Establishment: From Conservative Ideology to Political Power.* New York: Harper & Row, 1988. A notably objective and well-written interpretation of the rise of a conservative elite, from the "dark days" of the 1960s through the Reagan revolution.

Richard Bolton, ed.
: *Culture Wars.* New York: New Press, 1992. Documents from controversies in the arts during 1989-1990, including illustrations of representative graphics and performances; includes useful chronology.

Ward Churchill
: *Fantasies of the Master Race: Literature, Cinema and the Colonization of American Indians.* Monroe, ME: Common Courage Press, 1992. A bitter and incisive attack on cultural stereotyping and exploitation of Native Americans.

Sara Diamond
: *Spiritual Warfare: The Politics of the Christian Right.* Boston: South End Press, 1989. Extensive and well-documented investigative journalism on this movement's ideology, organization, and ties to large corporations.

Dinesh D'Souza
: *Illiberal Education: The Politics of Race and Sex on Campus.* New York: Vintage, 1992. An account of political correctness controversies at six universities, from a neoconservative perspective.

John Frohnmayer	*Leaving Town Alive.* Boston: Houghton Mifflin, 1993. Memoir of political infighting in Washington, by the chairman of the National Endowment for the Arts under Bush.
Gerald Graff	*Beyond the Culture Wars.* New York: Norton, 1992. A University of Chicago professor proposes that teaching the ideas of cultural conflicts can revitalize humanities education, and serve the best interests of students.
Robert T. Handy	*A Christian America: Protestant Hopes and Historical Realities.* New York: Oxford University Press, 1984. A professor of church history traces the efforts of mainline denominations to fully Christianize the U.S., including an overview of the colonial experience, but mostly dealing with the increasing pluralism of the late nineteenth and early twentieth centuries.
Robert Hughes	*Culture of Complaint: The Fraying of America.* New York: Oxford University Press, 1993. *Time* magazine art critic takes aim at both right and left who feed off each other for intellectual corruption; defends a centrist position.
James Davison Hunter	*Culture Wars: The Struggle to Define America.* New York: Basic Books, 1991. Traces historical origins of cultural conflict in America, arguing that a deep division has long existed between orthodox and progressive forces.
Tim LaHaye	*The Battle for the Mind.* Old Tappan, NJ: Revell, 1980. A leading conservative fundamentalist supports the Christianity vs. humanism, faith vs. atheism dichotomy in the modern world.
Meridel LeSueur	*Ripening.* New York: Feminist Press, 1990. Collection of essays by a veteran feminist writer who connects the heritage of midwestern socialist culture to radical movements today.
Erwin W. Lutzer	*Exploding the Myths That Could Destroy America.* Chicago: Moody Press, 1986. The senior pastor of the Moody Memorial Church exposes twelve myths, such as "We Can Have Morality Without Religion," and "The Church Should Have No Voice in Government."
Dave Marsh, et al.	*Fifty Ways to Fight Censorship.* New York: Thunder's Mouth Press, 1991. Short chapters on strategies to gather information on censorship, organizing freedom of speech and press campaigns; features lists of relevant addresses of music and bookstore chains, pressure groups, and civil liberties organizations.

Michael Medved	*Hollywood vs. America: Popular Culture and the War on Traditional Values.* New York: Harper-Collins, 1992. An attack on the entertainment industry that claims that Hollywood promotes violence and sexual decadence for profit.
Richard John Neuhaus, ed.	*Piety and Politics: Evangelicals and Fundamentalists Confront the World.* Washington, DC: Ethics and Public Policy Center, 1987. Documents, pro and con, concerning the movement for Christian political renewal.
Mark A. Noll, et al.	*The Search for Christian America.* Colorado Springs: Helmers & Howard, 1989. Three prominent scholars consider major issues in the "Christian nation" debate, including the experience of the Puritans, and the American Revolution.
Camille Paglia	*Sexual Personae: Art and Decadence from Nefertiti to Emily Dickinson.* New York: Vintage, 1991. An "audacious and learned work of guerrilla scholarship . . . making a persuasive case for all art as a pagan battleground."
Jonathan Rauch	*Kindly Inquisitors: The New Attacks on Free Thought.* Chicago: University of Chicago Press, 1993. Traces authoritarian attempts to regulate opinion back to Plato, and contends America faces a new Inquisition.
Pat Robertson	*The New World Order.* Successful Living Edition, 1991. The founder of the Christian Broadcasting Network (CBN) and host of "The 700 Club" updates the conspiracy theory of history, from the eighteenth-century Illuminati to the present.
Luis Rodriguez	*Always Running—La Vida Loca: Gang Days in L.A.* Willimantic, CT: Curbstone, 1993. An autobiographical account of gang life and culture, emphasizing hope and political struggle as the solution to urban problems.
Francis A. Schaeffer	*How Should We Then Live? The Rise and Decline of Western Thought and Culture.* Old Tappan, NJ: Revell, 1976. An influential evangelical philosopher interprets the broad outlines of European and American culture.
Herbert Schiller	*Culture, Inc.* New York: Oxford University Press, 1989. Contends that corporations have seized control of museums, theaters, performing arts centers, and public broadcasting stations.

Arthur M. Schlesinger Jr.	*The Disuniting of America.* New York: Norton, 1992. A prominent member of the "consensus" school of historians argues that "the cult of ethnicity" threatens our national identity.
Jay Sekulow	*From Intimidation to Victory: Regaining the Christian Right to Speak.* Lake Mary, FL: Creation House, 1990. The general counsel of Christian Advocates Serving Evangelism defends the legality of religious advocacy in education and public affairs.
Adam Sexton, ed.	*Desperately Seeking Madonna.* New York: Dell, 1993. Essays, cartoons, tabloid journalism, academic essays, comic book art "in search of the meaning of the world's most famous woman."
Rick Simonson, ed.	*Multi-Cultural Literacy.* St. Paul: Graywolf Press, 1988. Collection of essays on literacy and curriculum debates; includes a list of artists and concepts "for opening the American mind."
Page Smith	*Killing the Spirit.* New York: Viking Penguin, 1991. A prominent historian makes the case that the decline of American higher education is related to emphasis on research, rather than teaching; includes a summary of the development of universities in the U.S.
Charles J. Sykes	*Profscam: Professors and the Demise of Higher Education.* New York: St. Martin's Press, 1988. Charges that college teaching has become a lucrative racket, based on obscure research and pseudoscience.
Ferenc Morton Szasz	*The Divided Mind of Protestant America, 1880-1930.* University: University of Alabama Press, 1982. Demonstrates how the concepts of evolution and Biblical higher criticism provoked an alignment of liberals vs. conservatives.
Jack Weatherford	*Indian Givers: How the Indians of the Americas Transformed the World.* New York: Ballantine, 1988. Surveys a number of major contributions by American Indians, in agriculture, medicine, the formation of the world economic system, and the principles of democratic government.

Index

216